Carol

Enjoy

D0911219

mary

GOD EXPECTS ME

LIVING THE REALITY OF LIFE BY EMBRACING THE REALITY OF GOD

MARY "MAYME" BULGER

IHS PUBLISHERS

Saint Louis, Missouri

Copyright © 2015 by Mary Bulger. All rights reserved.

No part of this book may be reproduced in any form by any means, graphic, electronic, or mechanical, including photocopying, recording, taping or by any information storage retrieval system without the written permission of the publisher.

For permission requests, write to the publisher, addressed "Attention: Permissions Coordinator," at: gembymayme@gmail.com or online at www.gembymayme.com

Nihil Obstat:
Very Rev. Thomas W. Kunz, VE, JCD

Imprimatur:
Most Rev. David Allen Zubik
Bishop of Pittsburgh
February 16, 2015

The Nihil Obstat and the Imprimatur are declarations that this work is considered to be free from doctrinal or moral error. It is not implied that those who have granted the same agree with the contents, opinions, or statements expressed.

The Scripture quotations contained herein are from the New Revised Standard Version Bible: Catholic Edition copyright 1993 and 1989 by the Division of Christian Education of the National Council of the Churches of Christ in the U.S.A. Used by permission. All rights reserved.

Cover and Interior Design by Trese Gloriod - Design pro Christus (.com)

ISBN: 978-0-9847656-4-5

DEDICATED

To my God, with gratitude for this gift, I give it back to you, along with myself, to do as You will.

A MOST HONORABLE MENTION

To Husband, with love, admiration, and gratitude until death do us part, for having me and holding me from that day forward, through better and worse, through richer and poorer, through sickness and in health, for loving and cherishing. With God as my witness, I love you.

*A*CKNOWLEDGEMENTS

I give special thanks to my unsung advisors for your serious efforts and valuable time: thank you to Louise; thank you to Tom Jordan; thank you to Tom Murray; thank you to Lorraine Pollini; thank you to Karen Wyrem.

My deep gratitude goes to those with the eyes of the Church for taking precious time to review my manuscript and provide encouraging feedback, which refreshed my spirit: thank you to Bishop Paul Bradley; thank you to Sr. Yvonne Dursh; thank you to Fr. Joe Mele; thank you to Fr. John Rushofsky.

Thank you to Linda Manuel who was my loudest motivator when I stalled.

Thank you to Evy Severino for sharing talents and coaching me to "let go" and tackle my tasks with gusto.

Thank you to Joanie DeLuca for her gifts of time, energy, and an ear.

Thank you to Julia Wyrem for putting her graphic design skills to work on the website.

Thank you to all my pre-publication readers for humoring me while I handed out different versions of a work in progress for their reading pleasure and feedback.

Last, but not least, I thank Husband, Mom, my sisters and brothers, and my nieces and nephews for not balking at my sharing with the world their endearing selves.

*T*ABLE OF CONTENTS

PREFACE

Brushing God off as a young adult is not an uncommon occurrence. As teenagers, religious education seems a matter of academics like reading, writing, and arithmetic. Graduating high school is the permission slip to quit going to catechism classes. We leave home as fledglings seeking knowledge about everything and anything we find exciting. That does not often include higher education about God. Aspiring to become productive members of society, we grow up physically, mentally, and financially. Spiritually we remain childish. With this background, all too often, young adults embrace society's spin on the pursuit of happiness, quit going to church, and become distanced from God. Some of us return matter-of-factly once married or as parents wanting a beloved infant to be baptized. It's nothing personal. It's tradition.

Armed with only a teenager's perspective about God, Baby Boomers have children and grandchildren of Generation X and Generation Y (the Millennials) who follow the same religious lukewarm trend because their elders had very little spiritual knowledge to pass down.

As a Baby Boomer child, I was given the teachings of my Catholic faith, which I call the WHATs. Religiously educating the young in those days did not often include much detail or reasoning, which I call the WHYs behind the WHATs. Having no depth to my convictions, I had little interest in pursuing God as I left home and began life on my own. Needless to say, this "cradle Catholic" did not know our Creator very well.

I did not know what I did not know about God until I was in my thirties. Then I began to rekindle a rapport with Him based on childhood understandings. The relationship moved beyond a stagnant knowledge of Him into an active kinship with a very personal, deeply loving, heavenly Father. Our bond with God is meant to forever grow and develop in ways we cannot contemplate until we let Him take us there.

Our Father in Heaven expects us to seek Him sooner than later. This is not because He's egotistical or needs us to seek Him, but for our own health and well-being as a whole person, body and soul. He makes Himself known so we can find Him. My eventual understanding and acceptance of God as reality in daily living brought forth an epiphany worth sharing: Life is more peaceful and fulfilling not so much because we accept Him as our God, but more so when we treat Him as such – everyday – in everything.

Within these pages you will find pieces of yourself, friends, and family that hit home, whether it is where you have been, where you are, or where you want to go spiritually. Hopefully, *God Expects Me* encourages you to let our Lord share with you beyond what you know of Him. It is meant to urge you to accept, with confidence, His open invitation to lead you further into all He desires for you through Him. God Himself will provide assistance to move the mountains of doubt, boredom, confusion, anger, or the status quo illusion of faith that may keep one from pursuing unfamiliar territory. Like any evolving relationship, it takes two. God has an open line for each and every one of us 24/7, but a "yes" is necessary from our end to have a clear connection.

For more, call on Him. He's expecting you!

GOD EXPECTS ME

God Expects Me walks through many years of growing up in God. Each chapter begins with a Bible quotation as an acquired love of Scripture inspired my writing as well as my soul. From there, bits and pieces are given to relate how those old Bible stories and God's ways pertain to our every day, personal lives.

As much as possible, the pages unfold to portray an evolution from a child of God into an adult in chronological order. However, most chapters include more recent events and insights because they relate to that chapter's theme. Each is titled with respect to a lesson that promoted spiritual progression. Usually within a chapter, more than one incident is shared, all of which reflect an understanding of the overall conclusion. Each of those incidents may not directly relate to another. Therefore, I have sectioned them off by identifying them as "Eye-Opener #1" or "Eye-Opener #2" and so on. Hopefully, this format will allow you to perceive the maturing process within chapters as well as throughout the progression of the book.

This book spans a lifetime. Writing has taken place over about seven years. Some of the pages gushed forth like a waterfall. Some came smoothly like a pristine stream trickling steadily down on a sunny day. Others were more like well water that appears only after working hard at the pump with the hope that it hasn't dried up – in other words, with much contemplation and prayer. The "waterfall pages" took place within the first six months of writing. The "pristine stream" writing neatened up the mess of a gushing waterfall sprayed all over the place. I thought I was finished after the first year. As my prayer life and knowledge of my faith continued to mature, the "well water" pages also developed. Then I struggled with the original format of sharing personal experiences and humor versus incorporating history and guidance from the teachings of the Catholic Church. I opted to include some of all of it because all are gifts that contribute to spiritual development. Biblical record and the Church's wisdom give credence to God's work within a soul.

As you read, you are the "me" that *God Expects Me* reflects. It speaks of me, you, us, and every individual God has ever created in His image and likeness. May God bless and inspire every "me" who opens this book.

*Some names of friends and relatives have
been changed to respect privacy.*

INTRODUCTION

I know your works; you are neither cold nor hot. I wish that you were either cold or hot. So, because you are lukewarm, and neither cold nor hot, I am about to spit you out of my mouth. (REVELATIONS 3:15-16)

God wants a two-way commitment with everybody. It's called a covenant. He designs everyone to draw nearer because it's in our best interest. Corresponding to that natural desire, each person has the freedom to ignore or attend to that desire. For every child conceived, God has taken the first step toward inviting that unique individual into a love-filled, personal relationship unto Himself. I venture to say it sounds like spiritual *Facebook*. God takes the initiative to invite every single human to "friend" Him. Each must choose to confirm or to ignore the invitation. He knows there is a chance of rejection upfront, or one might "friend" Him only to "unfriend" Him at any time. The photo is missing, but His profile is unbelievably amazing. His philosophy is loud and clear. All the information needed to get to know God better is out there, but a decision to "log-in" must be made to get the facts and daily input. Participation is necessary to build a relationship.

Despite the prior lack of knowledge about God, He pulled me toward Him. When I chose to accept His invitation, *Facebook* did not exist. My initial move to know Him better was more like tracing a family tree. It was probably similar to Carl and Jan, friends living in Florida, who tracked their descendants, which sparked a great relationship with new-found relatives in Italy. The kinship became so stirring that they booked a vacation overseas to finally meet them. In essence, this is what happened when I delved into my religious heritage. God was at first an obscure relative to whom I didn't give much thought. Digging up the roots that tie me to the Father, Son, and Holy Spirit sparked in me a yearning to build an ever strengthening bond with Him.

We don't give it much thought, but most of us know people who are "neither cold nor hot" toward God. I was one of them. For the most part, I chose to ignore Him with a "not now" response. As a young adult, I believed He existed. I also knew the childhood basics about how He wanted me to live. For the record I was a Christian, but did not include Him in most aspects of life. I took Him for granted. He would have had every right to slap a "lukewarm" label on me because I carried on in life as if He didn't matter. I was both spiritually blasé and childish. It's the chicken or the egg debate. Did my lack of maturity lead to a lukewarm state or did my halfhearted faith block my entry into adulthood? Sadly, I was not alone. There are many tepid Christians. God only knows how many. One never admits to being lukewarm. It's not cool.

We also know people who are on fire for God. My friend Clara is a prime example. Her personality and way of life give gentle witness to a relationship with God that I would tag as "hot." Now in her nineties, she is a very spunky woman who has loved the Lord with all her heart from the time she was a child. She suffered with severe arthritis during childhood that left her bedridden. Her family holds onto the legacy that through devout prayer and faith, Clara was suddenly healed and was able to begin again the life of an active little girl. That experience of an overnight, miraculous answer to prayers triggered an unyielding faith that remains in her elderly heart until death does she part. Each and every day she commits time to retreat to her room to be alone with her Creator in silent prayer. Often in conversation Clara would remark "Where would I be without God?"

That brings us to those whom God might have a tendency to stick a "cold" label upon. My husband's brother Matt comes to mind. He was raised Catholic, but as he gained independence away from home he chose to abandon that faith. Matt was a successful pharmacist and an established atheist when I first met him over 25 years ago. He was the very first atheist I ever met; at least he was the first that identified as such. Digesting this fact about him, my brain immediately processed an inner thought confirming my belief in God. It hurt slightly that this man did not believe. I was miffed for all of two seconds and then forgot about it. Looking back, that twinge of offense strikes me as odd because, at the time, I had no enthusiasm for my faith either. I could offer no testimony to the reality of a supreme being, and yet something in me insisted that He existed. More recently, Matt has delved into literature on Eastern spirituality. His relationship with God is still "cold" in that he does not communicate at all with Him, but seeks spiritual power and control from his own person. He now maintains the philosophy that we are each gods within ourselves. My brother-in-law is a very intelligent man who expects hard evidence that one Almighty God exists before he would accept such a theory.

Matt had no faith to hand down to his two daughters when they were born. Neither did his wife tutor the children in any deep devotion before she separated herself from the family when the girls were young. His youngest daughter, Lori, is now 26 years old. She has been diagnosed as having a form of autism called Asperger's syndrome. She is very bright, but her social development has been stifled to that of a teenage girl. His oldest daughter, Kate, is presently 31 years old. When her mother left, Kate was 14 and fell into the role of mothering her little sister. It was a source of amazement to watch this adolescent nurture Lori in her special needs. While she was in her late teens, Kate and I had some conversations about life in general. I conveyed my observations that she was a very unselfish, loving young lady, and I was very proud of how she stepped up to help Lori. We also had a simple exchange about God. She could see that I possessed a deep faith. In order to connect with me in that way, Kate proudly proclaimed that she knew how to make the sign of the cross. Signing the cross is an act of faith and prayer easily taught to toddlers. My niece was mature in many ways, but her religious education was still in infancy. To date, she explores God by periodically making social visits with friends to varying places of worship. Her thermometer probably registers a tad above "lukewarm" because she dips into the idea of religion similar to the way youth date. She is flirting for the fun of it, but far from making a commitment.

My spouse and I also know a lovely, married couple Max and Lois who would accept the "cold" label to describe their relationship, or lack of, with God. Max was born in the early fifties in England and was raised Catholic. As a teen, he wasn't enthralled with the routine of being dropped off at church on Sundays. He was tall and looked much older than his 14 years. This advantage allowed him to walk from the church to a nearby pub, grab a pint, and relax for the better part of an hour. In a timely fashion, he'd head back to the church where his mum would pick him up. He got away with his weekly outing for some time. When his mother finally found him out, she gave him quite a physical reprimand for his sins. Some years later Max had a rude awakening when his mother quit attending Mass soon after his maternal grandmother passed away. Perhaps this double standard helped squash any conviction to his family's religious customs. Lois was also born in England, but was not Catholic. She attended a Catholic high school solely for the quality of education to be gained. Although the school required spiritual instruction, non-Catholics were given separate religious classes from the Catholic students.

Neither Max nor Lois developed a passion for the faith familiar to them. He is an atheist, and she is agnostic. Max teases me for my convictions with good humor while Lois asks questions about my unbelievable beliefs and awaits a reply. She does, though, view it as presumptuous to claim there is or isn't a supreme being for absolute certainty. The pair gently challenges me from a perspective not at peace with the existence of a Creator-God.

I have three brothers and six sisters. The oldest four, including me, uniformly drifted from our Catholic upbringing while the majority of the younger set kept the faith. My unscientific theory suggests that the different outcomes are based on different teaching styles. The first four were taught in an era when religious instruction was more like teaching math or English. We were given basic history and beliefs to remember, but an allowance for questioning was not built into the format. This manner of instruction instilled a "do as God says or you'll be punished" mentality. God the Father was a disciplinarian. I could relate to this image because my earthly father demonstrated both the method of not answering questions and the fear factor method by simply stating "because I said so." As schooling styles evolved, the youngest siblings were taught about God from a loving, fatherly perspective. This impression drew one nearer to Him simply for the sake of love rather than a fear of being punished. Eventually, I realized that God is the perfect melding of everything a father should incorporate. We tend to have difficulty conveying His perfection within our teaching methods as well as our own parenting styles.

My conclusion about teaching eras goes down the drain if looking at how my youngest brother drifted away despite being raised with "modern" teaching approaches. My husband is another exception to my rule. Three years my senior, he grew up in the former system, but he stuck with his convictions. He and Matt attended the same Catholic school, and were raised by parents in the same religious environment. Yet, for whatever reason, the brothers ended up on opposite ends of the belief spectrum.

The mentioned relatives and friends had varying degrees of exposure to religion while growing up. It is independence and freedom of choice that led several to abandon the idea of God, others to remain on the fence, and a number to keep their faith alive and well. Seeds were handed down and planted by parents, relatives, schools, books, and preachers in one combination or another. Some roots went deeper than others. Granted, some seeds are not given the best fertilizer in which to thrive. Those seedlings may lie dormant in the recipient for years, but someday curiosity may move a person to go on a fact-finding mission. That person may then choose to do their own sowing and grow those kernels into an adult relationship with God. If the seed is never planted, there is no option to develop it — or to let it die. God instilled a natural desire for us to seek Him, but an effort to cultivate that bond is needed to move one from cold, to lukewarm, to hot.

Examining my own religious evolution, the seeds of faith given to me by my parents tried to sprout, but I didn't feed them when I left childhood behind. They lay underdeveloped for many years. It is my experience that God initially fed those dormant seeds without my understanding of what was going on. His grace was alive within me, and He was courting me to gain attention. As an interest surfaced and then continued to grow, I set out to learn as much as possible about this God of mine. I was not just learning, but was entering into a relationship that continuously unfolded as each day passed. Over five decades of life, the mercury on my own spiritual thermometer has seen both extremes of temperature and everywhere in between. Within the last 20 years, I've seen myself grow consistently "hot."

Practically speaking, it is difficult to adequately express the joy and awe that accompany a "hot" attitude toward God. Such sentiment sounds illogical to someone with a "cold" faith in this Supreme Being. God comes across like a superhero in a fairy tale to a person that does not respond to Him. Faith prompts Christians to believe that this fairy tale is actually a non-fiction thriller. Hope leads us to believe it will end happily ever after because God wants all of us to share paradise with Him forever. Before we show up on His doorstep, however, He expects us to strive to live up to His expectations. At the same time, we are entitled to certain expectations of Him. True love builds this two-way arrangement between us and our Creator.

It took decades for me to commit to this exchange of friendship. I was stuck in a spiritual childhood and did not connect with God back in my youth. When people don't relate to Him, the gift of faith is pushed aside or left unopened. Specifically for those of us who find it hard to accept God solely on faith, He left humanity with a trail of history and teachings that fuel that gift with the ability to reason. If every person in the universe would pursue an adult education by following that trail, the lukewarm and the cold would heat up at an inspiring rate.

For me, it was after I began tracking that trail of faith that I quit taking God for granted and warmed up to Him. Little by little I learned about Him. It was slow going because I had no idea that what I was stepping into was so deep. I'm not the type of person that dives head first into a cold ocean to get the "freeze" over and done. Nope, I suffer by sticking my feet in the water and stand there shivering waiting to warm up before I go further. I expect Him to hold my hand while I hold my breath and put my face in the whole way. God knows I trust that He won't let me drown. He's by my side teaching me to swim, and I must choose every day to get in the water and go deeper. It is a daily choice that truly belongs to everyone.

Even after I began pursuing my connection with God, it took a while before I digested and became quite comfortable with the concept that He saw me on a very personal level. Acceptance of this mystery of a one-on-one bond was a trigger in the relationship, which put a new log on the fire. Still today, when I stop to think about God paying attention to every word I say, actually listening to me, actually seeing me and knowing me, and claiming me as the daughter He loves, I sit before Him in awe.

GOD EXPECTS ME TO BE HIS CHILD

Pray then in this way: Our Father in heaven. (MATTHEW 6:9)

In the days of Abraham, it was by way of circumcision that people entered the family of God. Jesus was circumcised when he was eight days old in accordance with His Father's covenant law with Abraham. As an adult, Jesus began teaching the Gospel and made it known that God's family is meant to include all people, not just the circumcised and their households. He introduced baptism as the new circumcision. Christ commissioned His Apostles to go:

> *Make disciples of all nations, baptizing them in the name of the Father and of the Son and of the Holy Spirit, and teaching them to obey everything that I have commanded you. (MATTHEW 28:19-20)*

For over 2000 years to this day, followers have entered into the Father's covenant family in this manner.

Jesus was an infant when He was presented to His Father in the temple. I was an infant when my parents presented me to God at my christening. As Christ instructed, I was baptized in the name of the Father and of the Son and of the Holy Spirit. God was now officially my Father as I ceremoniously became His tiny daughter.

EYE-OPENER #1: *Being baptized a child of God does not mean we automatically know Him as our Father.*

In order to convey various stages of spiritual growth and maturity within *God Expects Me*, it may be helpful to first provide some of my background. You most likely have similar memories, especially if you were born and raised Catholic somewhere within the last 50 to 60 years. That covers a lot of us.

Born and baptized in the late fifties, I am the third of ten children. My upbringing was as a true "cradle Catholic" including six years of Catholic grade school. I remember going to Mass every morning, making my first Confession and Communion, praying the rosary, participating in the May crowning ceremony, and obeying the rule to wear a hat in church. If I forgot my hat, I would run into the girl's room, grab a paper towel and expertly bobby pin it to my hair. I was now prepared for Mass. In those early years, my physical and spiritual developments were in balance.

As a child, I loved God with all my heart even though I didn't truly relate to Him as a heavenly Father. He was more like Santa Claus. He had a Heaven 'n Hell list and was checking it twice to find out who was naughty or nice. I understood God to be in charge of the entire universe. He was similar to the President of the United States because He had an awfully big job to do for all people, but He didn't relate one on one. I don't recall praying strictly for myself, but it was an automatic activity to pray to God when something was wrong or someone needed help. Standard prayers included family things such as: *please let Grandpa get better; please let Jasper (my cat) come home; please let my parents win at the church raffle;* and *please don't let my family get killed in a car crash.* Answering prayers came with the territory of being the Almighty. My prayers were to God, never to Jesus. I didn't quite "get" Jesus Christ. I knew the basics. Christ was God's Son. He suffered and died on a cross for sins so that I could go to Heaven if I was nice. My little mind didn't go beyond those basic truths. I matter-of-factly accepted that I received

His body and blood in the Eucharist, but He was not an emotional element of my childhood. Unlike the Apostles in the Bible, I never saw a tongue of fire hovering over my head signifying the presence of God the Holy Spirit (Acts 2:1-4). Therefore, besides not relating fully to Jesus, I was not prompted to ask the Spirit to guide my life. I did not grasp these three Persons of the Trinity.

Armed with a strong desire to be good and Heaven-bound, I was well on my way to sainthood for the first 12 years of life. I talked to God about everything my family needed. One miraculous prayer event took place in the fifth grade. It was the last day of school before summer vacation and the class was celebrating. Two homemade cakes were being raffled before dismissal. There were 21 students in my class including my sister, Jean. Pieces of paper holding all of our names went into a hat. Everyone gathered round for the drawing and as naturally as breathing, I closed my eyes tightly and began praying. My prayer was from the innocent heart of a child. It was an appeal meant to bring a joyful surprise to a big family where money was always tight. *Dear God, please let me or Jean win a cake. It would be so neat to have dessert after supper when it's not even Sunday.* I prayed over and over and over until the first name was drawn. I won; it was a miracle! The second name was drawn. It was my sister's; we had a double miracle! God's all-knowing abilities allowed Him to understand that one single-layer cake was not enough to feed a family the size of a baseball team, including management. I closed my eyes to thank Him for dessert. Then I apologized for praying too much.

Grace was said every evening at dinner. That was the extent of formal prayer time. Living in a household of 12 did not leave time or energy for my parents to gather us for family prayer. Their faith, hope, and love flowed by working and struggling to support the den, constantly caring for toddlers, cooking for the brood, getting kids off to school, refereeing breaches in peace, making sure those eligible got to religion class, confessions, and after school stuff. Every Sunday we took up an entire pew as the family attended Mass together. Mom encouraged us on a nightly basis to remember to say our prayers at bedtime. Christian morals were taught at home and at Catholic grade school. The teaching was on a "thou shalt not" basis rather than a deep spiritual connection as to why God deemed it best we do this and not that for our own health and happiness. As children, we obeyed the rules - most of us - most of the time. Each grew wise enough to realize we could sometimes get away with law breaking. Take for example my brother, John, whose wit spared him punishment for using a swear word. At about the age of nine, he angrily used "Hell" during a rant. After being ratted out by a sibling, John offered his defense to Mom that he did not curse because he only pronounced one "L."

Entering public school in seventh grade did not nourish my faith. In fact, the years spent there were the catalyst for my break-up with God. My demise can be traced all the way back to a fellow grade-school classmate. She left Catholic school and was infiltrated into the public system several years before I arrived. This girl was a brute and had what it took to be a "hood." Nevertheless, I was convinced she was my friend, so I did not question her demeanor. She smoked cigarettes, showed me an "adult" magazine once, and always covered the Blessed Mother statue in her bedroom with a white sheet when her mom wasn't looking. One day just as ninth grade English class was about to begin, my instigator friend grabbed my purse and began rummaging through it. She pulled out a small plastic-encased card bearing my name, address, phone number, and a plea to call a priest in case of an emergency. (Mom thought it a good idea for me to carry it.) She waved the certificate around and loudly proclaimed that I was Catholic, and the class must call a priest should I start to die. Although I was dying of embarrassment, a priest never showed up. I threw away the plastic, priest plea and quit talking to God. Suffering for Him was not a concept I was ready to accept.

Being the only driver in the household, Dad drove us to Sunday school each week with devotion. These obligatory evening catechism classes bored me during my high school years. When my oldest sibling turned 16, he got his driver's license and took over this shuttle duty. Now we had the liberty of skipping class to hang out at Burger King. That was fine by me because I reasoned that I knew all I needed to know. God expected me to grow up into an adult spiritually as well as physically, but I didn't. I continued to age physically while my understanding of Him stagnated.

Growing up as the third oldest had advantages. There wasn't much time for one-on-one conversation with parents fending for younger siblings, but I did become semi-independent early on. Babysitting and a newspaper route helped me become money savvy, which allowed me to purchase cool clothes and paraphernalia that any teenage girl should own. After high school, I attended the community college, worked evenings at a clothing store, and waitressed on weekends. A required portion of my earnings went to pay the piper – my parents. Helping Mom in the kitchen and with cleaning and laundry would all come in handy when it came time for me to move out on my own. After two years at the college, I had an associate's degree in liberal arts, which only prepared me for more college. At the age of 19, a higher education seemed less important than earning money, so I took a full-time job as a secretary at a large university. Commuting on the public transit system for an hour ride to and from work became tiresome. It was time. I moved into an apartment conveniently located near the university. Dad was sweet to help me move into my new place. His eagerness may have stemmed from knowing the household budget would ease a bit if one of the fold was feeding herself.

For at least the first year away from home, I continued to go to church on Sundays. Not understanding Mass from an adult spiritual vantage, I still attended because it was one of the rules. It became apparent very quickly that not many people my age living away from home went to church. Nor did they talk much about God, if at all. As time went by, it became easier not to go to Mass – if I had another obligation, if it was raining, if I was tired. It was easy not to go.

At age 20, I became seriously ill with pneumonia and was hospitalized for 10 days. My prognosis worsened before it became better. A very high fever caused me to hallucinate, and I became paranoid that "they" were trying to kill me. My sister, Josie, walked a few miles from the nearby technical school she attended to visit me each day. I regret that I cannot remember a single time. It was only during a recent conversation with my brother, Will, that I learned he also came to see me in the hospital. (This is worthy of mention because back then I didn't think Will knew he had me for a sister.) Being so sick and on antibiotics repeatedly while recovering wreaked havoc on my system. Eventually I gained my health and energy back. I survived.

After hitting the 21 milestone, I began a new job in the corporate work force. Shortly after the job transition, I was physically attacked in the hallway leading to my apartment. The attacker ran off with my purse after I screamed. I suffered minor cuts and bruises, but having a butcher knife held to my throat, being threatened with rape, and punched in the face changed my happy-go-lucky attitude. No longer would I trust everyone and their brother. Naturally, I opted to move away from my city dwelling into a smaller, safer, old-town neighborhood. It was in this "safer" environment that my apartment was broken into, my car stolen twice, and later vandalized in a separate incident. Again seeking a safer haven, I moved a few miles away into a second-floor apartment. This move must have been a wise decision because there I only experienced one failed break-in attempt. I survived.

At age 23, I had surgery twice for a malignant melanoma. Left untreated, this type of skin cancer spreads to inner organs where it is often fatal within five years. Fortunately, mine was diagnosed early enough to treat successfully. The second surgery removed all cancer cells, and I did not need to endure chemotherapy or radiation treatment. I survived.

Packing these struggles into a few short years festered into some anxiety issues. Going it alone without an active faith did not help me cope. What faith I had was not shaken, however, because I did not have that personal connection with our Father who art in Heaven. I had a subconscious opinion that life was just happening, and God had no involvement. My childhood habit of praying for others, but not myself, was deep-seated. It never dawned on me to pray in any of these situations. Back then, it was Mom who did the praying for me. Today I'm confident He heard her prayers.

While living my teens and twenties, I did not recognize God working in my life. It stood to reason that I had not yet claimed Him as my Father.

EYE-OPENER #2:   *God can be taught in a child's curriculum, but the relationship won't fully bloom until the child matures into a mutually loving bond with Him.*

Some traditionally have children baptized in infancy. Others think it best to be baptized as an adult after a person makes his or her own choice to participate in the family of God. Some think of baptism as forcing a baby to enter into a religious faction when they cannot consent. My two cents in the matter is that responsible parents make many choices for their infant, their toddler, their teenager. They do so in the best interest of the child. I liken infant baptism to that of parents blanketing up their precious one to protect him or her from cold, harsh weather. Adults first wash a baby clean, and then they bundle up the tiny tot because the child is unable. Baptism spiritually cleanses an infant who is then spiritually bundled into the palms of our heavenly Father. The blanket can be kept or thrown off as a child becomes a decision-making adult. All of us have the freedom to deny our heavenly heritage.

Teaching religious convictions to children in general is also met with differing opinions. Some consider instructing youngsters about one religion over another as brainwashing. The reasoning is that little ones typically believe anything without question. Yes, children are very accepting of all they are taught, but brainwashing implies using unethical means to control someone in a way that deters independent thinking. Certainly, brainwashing can occur in the religious arena as much as it occurs in political, personal, financial, sexual, domestic, or educational matters. Customarily, though, I don't view instructing children in spiritual beliefs as brainwashing. Offspring routinely inherit viewpoints, along with such things as: names, moral codes, life skills, money, and property. All are provided because loving relatives strive to hand down what they accept as good. Responsible parents educate children in matters valuable enough to allow their young to go off to lead independent, productive lives. This includes sharing a faith held up as being important, normal, good, and vital for well-being. Conscientious mentoring encourages kids to think, to build upon what they have been given, and to someday pass along wisdom to their own offspring. Hopefully, a child raised by such parents will go off into adulthood able to make wise decisions. Among those decisions is to accept or reject the faith of their forefathers. In choosing, we opt individually, consciously or subconsciously, to have or not have a relationship with God.

Let's take me for example. I was a by-the-book Catholic baby who was baptized and religiously educated as an outpouring of my parents' love. It was when I was baptized that I first received the gift of the Holy Spirit even though I was unaware He existed. The Spirit flows forth from the loving bond of God the Father and Jesus the Son to guide us in our relationship with God throughout our lives. As a teen, under the direction of my parents and the Church, I received the sacrament of Confirmation. This was the designated age when I was presumed mature enough to renew my baptismal vows, accept the Holy Spirit on my own behalf, and confirm acceptance of the covenant relationship between me and God. Even so, a year or two later as my independent thinking skills kicked in, I began to lose interest in Him. Moving into young adulthood, I threw off the blanket of baptism my parents had wrapped me in and stuffed it under the sofa. I made my own decision to leave it there and allow it to darken with dust bunnies. Though I received the Spirit at baptism, and acknowledged Him at Confirmation, it was a gift I pushed aside with a lack of understanding. The gift of the Spirit is like a mechanical toy a child receives on a birthday. If the little tyke doesn't know how to utilize the toy, he or she may or may not learn to put the gift to proper use. For a long time, I let the Spirit idle in me while He waited for me to acknowledge Him. In due course, I would make the decision to wash off my blanket and cloak myself in it again. That didn't truly happen within my heart until I was in my mid-thirties. This is when I initially felt that want to be His child, and I began praying for His Spirit to be active within me. Ultimately, I reclaimed my place in God's family and learned to call Him my Father.

During my younger days, I did not understand or relate well to the Trinity. Therefore, I am including a basic explanation of God the

Father, the Son, and the Holy Spirit[1] to assist anyone who grapples with the concept as I did. Words cannot capture the full understanding of the mystery of the Blessed Trinity, but my attempt follows:

> Christians worship one divine God. He has three Persons within the same divine nature, which is God. He reveals Himself to us in different ways within these three Persons:

> First, He reveals himself as our Father, the Creator. In His image, we were created with and for love to enjoy eternal life with Him. We have a spiritual soul, which has the built-in goodness of God.

> Secondly, God reveals himself as the Son in the Person of Jesus Christ. Jesus is known as the Savior. He is God who became man when He was miraculously born in our image of flesh. At the same time, Jesus maintains His divine nature as God. He suffered, died, was buried, and rose from the dead to fulfill God's will that we may have eternal life.

> Thirdly, God reveals himself as the Holy Spirit who proceeds from the love of the Father and Son. The Spirit carries forth what the Father and Son have handed down as He guides, counsels, strengthens, and comforts us so that we, too, may carry forth God's will for the sake of His family.

> As humans, we can relate to each Person accordingly and call on each as our hearts and minds direct. At the same time, we can be confident that if we pray to one Person of the Trinity, we are listened to and answered by all three as one God.

---

1 "The Catechism of the Catholic Church" is an excellent source for a more in-depth summary of the Trinity. The official Vatican website (www.vatican.va) conveniently has the entire Catechism available online for access to Church teachings. It is my suggestion that the official Vatican website be consulted to verify information obtained by other sources.

In terms of human relationships, we can only skim the surface of the concept of three Persons in one God. Despite the disadvantage of using my own words and mentality to explain the supernatural, I'll consider my own interactions with people. In my bonds with others I am a daughter, a sister, a wife, a friend, an employee, a co-worker, an aunt, and a Godmother. I have all these responsibilities rolled up into one woman. Depending on the situation, my role changes, and I reveal a different side of myself. My demeanor adjusts when conversing with a niece or nephew versus one of my good friends. I try to be more of a mentor with my Godchildren instead of the smart aleck I am with my sisters. While talking to a stranger, I'm likely to be more reserved in speech than with my husband. I use assorted aspects of my being to interact with and respond to those who know me. I am one woman revealed in many ways at the appropriate times. The Trinity is one God revealing Himself to us in three different Persons appropriately. This is how we come to know our one God completely; at least as completely as our human understanding allows.

The problem with my analogy is that my various, distinct roles stem from within only one human personality. God has revealed himself in different roles within three definite, distinct, supernatural Persons.

GOD EXPECTS ME TO LIVE IN THE WORLD, NOT BE "OF THE WORLD"

Do not be conformed to this world, but be transformed by the renewing of your minds, so that you may discern what is the will of God — what is good and acceptable and perfect.
(ROMANS 12:2)

EYE-OPENER #1: *Our culture makes it difficult to be in tune with God's desires for His people.*

What really wore on my mental and spiritual health was the urban, corporate arena. During the early eighties, the office mindset was suggestive of a downtown party atmosphere. Prior to moving away from home, I was fairly sheltered from most of the world. Those 15-minute TV soap operas I watched in the summer while folding laundry with Mom did not prepare me for the big city. Within this business backdrop, I met people who were literally living soap operas, but their scripts would have been edited out of the soaps of yesteryear due to the risqué content. "Sexual harassment" had not been named yet, but it was alive and well in corporate America. Fortunately for me, my immediate supervisors always proved to be respectful, true mentors. However, there were plenty of older, wiser, established, married men offering to lead me into compromising positions. I was young enough to not know I could reprimand these mature, executive offenders, but old enough not to want to appear like a child. So, I played it cool and acted like it didn't happen. That didn't make it go away. Extra-marital affairs seemed common place with no apparent need to hide it. The voice in my new environment was shouting that it was a rite of passage to have multiple and casual lovers, to lie, to cheat, to break up families, and hearts all at the same time. Alcohol was a lunchtime staple and drugs were weekend recreation. My head was swimming with new concepts about the way the world worked. Exposure to these alternative activities day after day led me to become numb to what certainly would make it onto the "thou shalt not" list.

Without education and a strong conviction about what God expects, familiarity can breed indifference, and even acceptance, as immoral and unhealthy behavior becomes the norm versus the exception. It happened to Moses' ancestors before they were freed from slavery in Egypt. Prior to becoming slaves, the Hebrew people were faithful to God's ways. However, generations of bondage in Egypt allowed the Egyptian gods and rather unscrupulous social behaviors to creep into the lives of His chosen people. They became desensitized. It became acceptable conduct among the Hebrews even though their one, true God did not approve of such goings on. The invitation into my own ancient Egypt by new acquaintances, friends, and co-workers was too tantalizing to ignore. I stepped through the looking glass and became of the world. I lost my eyes, my ears, and my voice, but I fit in just fine.

My anxieties climbed as I became accustomed to this new world. I didn't make any connection between being so mixed up and living against the principles I was taught as a child. Barely into my twenties, my physician recommended that I talk to a psychologist. This counselor looked to be fresh out of college with only book learning to cure me. He was able to see things quite clearly from where he sat, and he shared his worldly insight. Never mind the spiritual aspect, let's go with Freud's take on existence. He brought me to see that I was too uptight about enjoying life. No need to be apprehensive. According to the doctor, it was important to let myself relax and take in all that life had to offer. My days would apparently be less stressful if I followed the credo "when in Rome, do as the Romans do." Off I went. I had the permission of a professional to be free not only in my personal ancient Egypt, but Rome as well!

I muzzled my conscience while trying to be carefree. My anxiety increased while traveling in directions against my natural judgment of what God found acceptable. My childhood take on "thou shalt not" was embedded in me, but I was not a born leader. Inwardly, I questioned what was going on around me. Outwardly, I never challenged the world. I knew the rules, the WHATs, God expected me to follow, but I didn't know the WHYs behind His ways. Because I did not have a deep understanding of why those rules were beneficial to true health and happiness, the WHATs had no value to me. They didn't stick. Knowing only the WHATs, and not the WHYs, did not make me strong enough to go out and live His teachings. Instead of "finding myself" from the depths of who I was, I blended into the times by conforming to social trends. Conforming is natural when one lacks the confidence or knowledge to consider God's take on life in comparison to society's. I was a tried and true follower. Since then, I've wondered how different my decisions might have been had I involved God. Now, I pray for the up-and-coming young adults fitting into today's times, hoping they will take Him personally soon, not later. Requesting wisdom from God in life's decision-making process can make all the difference in deciding wisely.

EYE-OPENER #2: *God "graces us" in our ignorance, inviting us in His direction.*

Aspiring to become a model in my early twenties, I seriously built a portfolio and pursued my dream over several years. I enjoyed a small bit of success acquiring advertising print work and runway assignments through local designers. The reward for me was the satisfaction of doing what I set out to do. One of my fondest memories during those days was briefly meeting Eileen Ford, the founder of the internationally famous Ford Modeling Agency in New York City. The year was 1981. She was conducting "cattle call" interviews at a downtown department store as part of a worldwide model search. No way was I going to miss the chance of a lifetime to meet Mrs. Ford. I decided to stay in town after work to attend the event. The waiting line was long and full of teenage girls, but I expected as much. It did not daunt me to wait my turn for over an hour before finally reaching this stately woman. She smiled and asked me my name. I replied. Then she asked how old I was. I was 23 at the time, although I looked younger. She smiled again and took my hand. She looked at my wrist and told me I was very thin. Then she patted my hand and said, "You would have made a terrific model. Why didn't you start sooner?" My explanation was that I didn't know how to go about it when I was a teen, and my parents would not have been able to assist financially. Mrs. Ford asked me to go to the makeup counter in the store, tell them she sent me over, and ask the makeup artist to "do" my lips. I thanked her, stepped away, and went toward the counter. Before reaching it, I looked at my watch. The next public transit bus was scheduled to arrive in 15 minutes; not enough time to have cosmetics applied, go back to show Mrs. Ford, and still catch my usual ride home. If I stayed, I would have an additional 30 minutes before the next bus. Waiting the extra half hour was not long in the scheme of things, nor was it uncommon for me to miss one bus and wait for another. Only about five seconds went by between the glance at my watch and the decision to catch my ride sooner than later. Considering how passionate I was about pursuing modeling and talking to Mrs. Ford, my actions did not make sense. It strikes me as odd that there was no emotion or regret about the choice to ignore her instructions. Looking back at that decision, I can't help but wonder if the Spirit of God was guiding me though I did not ask for His help. That was a period in time when the lifestyles of some famous models were riddled with drugs and other destructive habits. Being more of a follower, I could envision getting into trouble had I been determined to chase my dream in New York. Knowing how much my mother prayed for her children, I now see her prayers as being answered in the form of graces that steered me from going deeper into the world's embrace and further from God's.

GOD EXPECTS ME TO KEEP HOLY THE LORD'S DAY

Remember the Sabbath day, and keep it holy. (EXODUS 20:8)

It has been said many times by many people that "You don't have to go to church to talk to God." The problem with this logic is that it implies that talking to God would indeed take place, just not within the walls of a church. It is my experience that I did not keep holy the Lord's Day inside or outside of a church. The truth is that I didn't know God well enough to want to worship Him one way or another. Therefore, I did not bother much. Adopting the "Don't have to go to church to talk to God" motto gave me a doctor's excuse for skipping Mass.

In 1983, my baby sister, Rebecca, asked me to be her Confirmation sponsor. Following protocol, I sought approval to do so from the priest at the parish where I was registered. He asked if I regularly attended Sunday Mass. Uh oh. Despite my aptitude for breaking commandments since leaving home, I found it downright difficult to lie to a priest. I replied with a truthful "no." This led Father to proclaim that he would not sign paperwork allowing me to be a sponsor. After further conversation, and my promise to go back to church, he gave his approval. I kept my promise and attended Mass regularly. Honestly, I did. For awhile.

In December of 1985, I met the man who would become my husband. Rarely did I call him by his given name, but took to calling him "Mister." At this point, depending on which way the wind was blowing, my attendance at church was sporadic again. Once Mister and I started dating on a regular basis, we began going to Sunday Mass together at his invitation. It was thoroughly enjoyable sitting next to my boyfriend and holding hands in the pew. Physically, I attended. Spiritually, I was uninvolved.

EYE-OPENER #1:   *Worshipping God at Mass is a sacred grace and is for our sake, not His.*

Even though I was attending Mass again each Sunday, it took quite a few more years before I became emotionally involved. Eventually, I gained a knowledge and understanding of the celebration of Mass and the Eucharist (Holy Communion), which drew me to church for the opportunity to worship God and be with Jesus. Participating in Mass became the most sacred way for me to adore Him while obeying the commandment to keep holy the Lord's Day. I grew to appreciate that as a member of His family, worshipping in church allowed me to unite with other members as a community. Yes, I can worship and pray anywhere, but going to Mass was the only place I could receive the sacrament of Holy Communion. Although private prayer time became a precious part of my relationship with God, I matured to realize that no amount of communing with Him outside of Mass can give me that same physical, miraculous union with Christ as in the Eucharist. Prior to getting to this appreciation of worship, I would first experience many lessons about prayer, the Mass, the Eucharist, and God as my relationship with Him slowly developed.

EYE-OPENER #2:   *Lukewarmness is a common struggle in growing up.*

A wild guess tells me that all of us know at least one friend or relative who quit going to church for one reason or another. My lack of spiritual emotion led me to back away from Mass in my early twenties. A generation later, I know more than a few young adults who have made that same decision at even younger ages. It does not seem that any of us spitefully ignore God, but we are halfhearted about becoming involved in the relationship. Even though there are many believers in God, there exists this lack of interest because we just don't get to know Him well at all.

I see my younger self reflected in my lovely niece, Kelsey, who recently graduated college. She was raised Catholic and attended her parish's school through eighth grade. Every Sunday before going off to college she would attend Mass with her family. She continued that practice in her first semester as a freshman, but somewhere along the line she quit attending. Most likely, stealing time for little luxuries, such as relaxing, accommodating a social life, and sleeping in on weekends all played a part in her decision not to go to church. There is also a lack of understanding regarding the Eucharist as the highlight of keeping the Lord's Day for a reverent Catholic. Based on experience, I surmise that she has not obtained a deeper, personal comprehension of her faith. Although her relationship with God is stilted, she has proved to be compassionate and loving toward others. During school breaks, she would coordinate student service projects or work as an assistant at a home for the mentally challenged. It is in this role of caring for adults with varying degrees of disability that I see Kelsey as a rare breed. It takes a very special person to attend to the needs of those having little awareness of social graces and physical control. In her work, her heart reflects the image of her Creator. An intelligent young woman, she is sensible about earning money toward her continuing education and balances her job, studies, and social life. I can relate to the ease with which my niece has backed away from her childhood beliefs. She was rooted in the faith, but those roots have not fully sprouted. Intuition tells me Kelsey will someday desire to nurture that faith and enter spiritual adulthood. She might then look for answers, find them, and embrace our Lord once again in a way she does not yet fathom.

CHAPTER 4

GOD EXPECTS ME
TO INVITE HIM INTO
ANYTHING AND EVERYTHING

Do not worry about anything, but in everything by prayer and supplication with thanksgiving let your requests be made known to God. (PHILIPPIANS 4:6)

I broke up with Mister three times during our dating relationship. Each time I missed him terribly, so I would return to say I'm sorry. He took me back with open, loving arms. God does the same thing if we walk away and want to return. He would welcome one back indefinitely while I'm not sure how many more times Mister would have echoed God's compassion.

My back and forth church-going patterns could be compared with the way my father saw my dating habits. Two years into the courtship, Dad slipped in some rare fatherly advice. One Saturday afternoon, I stopped home to find him downstairs working in his shop where he was a self-employed dog groomer. He went about his business clipping a stately miniature Schnauzer, and I sat in the visitor's chair to visit. We chatted about how my car was running and then about how Mister was doing. Obviously, two years was way too long to have a relationship without a true commitment because Dad said, "You know, Daughter, I think it's about time for that boyfriend of yours to either shit or get off the pot." God may have been thinking the same thing about my commitment to Him, but I'm sure He would have cleaned up the language. Six months after my father shared his advice, I stopped by and proudly announced that Mister "shat." Dad was very pleased that my boyfriend was now my fiancé.

EYE-OPENER #1: *Invite God into the lifelong things.*

About a week after accepting Mister's proposal, I did something odd. At least for me it was odd. I took a moment out of my workday to silently pray, *If I'm supposed to marry Mister, let it be. If he is not the man I'm to marry, then give me the courage to say no.* Prior to this prayer, I felt I had taken control of life. I had a good job; I was independent; I paid my bills promptly; I was attending evening classes to earn a bachelor's degree; my employer was paying the tuition; I was able to help my family when the need arose; I had friends, a social life, and fun. In my assessment, I didn't need anything including a need to talk to God. Obviously, I was capable of making my own decisions. I could take care of myself, thank you. Making this decision to get married was different. I was in control, but I was not confident in the whole "until death do us part" love concept. Mister and I had lots of fun together, but how was I supposed to know if this was "it," if this was the one, true love of my life that would be defined by forever? For that moment, that day, my childhood faith to trust God took over. That instinct moved me to pray my first direct, heart-felt, sincere prayer in adult life. I invited God to guide me with this lifelong decision.

On February 18, 1989 Mister became my husband. Keeping up with tradition, I did not call my love by his given name. He was still Mister to me, but I also began calling him "Husband." This was confusing for one of our preschool nieces because she had come to know him as Uncle Mister.

As Mr. and Mrs., we were on the road to happily-ever-after, which meant understanding that well-traveled roads have bumps. Periodically, Husband would comment that he was third in my life. I did not accept his statement until years gone by, but eventually understood his meaning. Work was my priority during the week. On weekends, he was pushed into third place while I caught up on chores, errands, and with the many social events, worries, and goings on that stem from a large family. At one point, Husband was bumped down another rung on the ladder when we got our first puppy together. He readily accepted that rung.

Yes, I had asked God for help in my decision to accept Mister's marriage proposal, but immediately went back to my bad habit of not talking to Him until the next time I needed something. When I wed my Husband, I barely invited God to the wedding, and Husband took Him more seriously than I did. For me, it was out of tradition and expectation that I routinely accepted a church wedding in our plans. At 30 years old, my spiritual maturity was very much out of balance with my physical age. No, I still did not talk much to God or about Him. My sister, Erin, must have noticed that He was not a high priority in my life because she offered some advice. She simply mentioned that marriage is not always easy, and to improve the chances of it thriving, God should be invited into it. Her words were tucked into my memory bank.

So as not to leave you hanging, I'll jump ahead for a moment to let you know that Husband and I now have 26 years of marital training under our belt. As we continuously grow through marriage, I have no doubt God answered that heart-felt prayer I made so long ago and approved my choice for a husband. Very often, I have thanked Him for the gift of my spouse. That is not to say that life is guaranteed perfect after promising "I do." One of my favorite wall plaques hangs in our kitchen reminding us every day, "This marriage was made in heaven, but so was lightning and thunder" (Author unknown). Instigator that I am, I take this opportunity to admit that once or twice I have asked my heavenly Father to exchange my gift. To be fair, Husband has had moments when he would have gladly given up marriage for a less stressful status. I came with a no-return policy. God has the same policy for each one of us based on His unconditional love.

EYE-OPENER #2:   *Invite God into the emergencies.*

People perceived me as such a calm person, but my insides were riddled with anxieties. I hid it quite well most of the time, but my mind was frequently in turmoil. All of that inner unrest was carried into our marital union, but I did not address it. So, I went about life as usual, and nobody knew I was slowly melting. The truth was that I cried a lot on the sly and had panic attacks. My emotional state also suffered at the hands of food allergies and unbalanced hormones, both of which had the power to alter my moods if not monitored. My worst eating habits were on the weekends. I could eat all the junk food I wanted and still have time to recover before heading back to work on Mondays. On any given Saturday or Sunday, the effects of my weekend pattern turned me into Hyde rather than the good Dr. Jekyll normally portrayed. I would roll out of bed grouchy. My husband was innocently downstairs having coffee and reading the paper. I would join him, but brought with me an unpleasant aura. Mister always rode out the storms.

One Saturday morning, I was in a particularly blue mood. Husband was out running errands while I retreated to the bedroom to cry with no need to explain. This was not an ordinary cry. It was deep, anguished, and desolate. Words cannot describe what was going on in my mind as I buried tears in the pillow. However, some things were clear: the world was a cruel place; crime and murder were rampant; children were being abused more often than not; one of my brothers was a manic depressive; my parents struggled constantly; and there was no point to it all. For someone having no emotional involvement with God, I was quite bold to declare that everything was entirely His fault. He was in charge of the universe, yet He didn't lift a finger to clean up the mess His people made. What is the point of praying? What is the point of living? Still sobbing, I went ahead and did that odd thing again – I prayed from the heart. I got up off the bed and knelt down on the floor. Out loud, from the bottom of my being, I looked up at the ceiling and spat out, *Is this it? Is this all there is?* Instantaneously, I stopped crying. My eyes closed in unknown prayer and a smile replaced my tears. My entire body was enveloped in a "pins and needles" sensation. I experienced total peace. Despite my stagnant relationship with God, I was quite aware that it was He. God had given me a hug.

For days, all I could think about was that embrace, but I didn't know what to do with it. Never had I heard of anyone else receiving such a hug, which made me doubt it was real. I didn't get the deeper meaning of my heavenly experience right away, so I ignored it. At this stage of my life, I was convinced that if I mentioned this to anyone, it would confirm insanity. I ignored it, but I never forgot it. Years later, I made sense of that encounter. God had graced me with His presence through His Spirit. He heard my desperate cry and made sure I knew He was listening. It didn't matter that I was yelling at Him. It mattered that I spoke from my heart. It mattered that I invited Him into my mess that day. God's hug answered my question, "Is this all there is?" with a firm "No. There is more. I AM." He made it clear that I must invite Him into my life in order to possess that inner peace no matter how dire the circumstance seems.

EYE-OPENER #3: *Invite God into the little things.*

One of the simple, fun things that I invited God into was to help Husband and I adopt a dog. We were mourning the death of our dog, Finnigan, and missed him terribly. The house was empty and our routines so different without him. I wanted another dog right away, but Husband wanted to wait. We compromised and decided to put off getting another pet for six months. I agreed to the delay only after Husband joked that, based on my hurry to replace Finnigan, he could picture me racing to find a date to escort me to his funeral someday.

Waiting six months was easier said than done. Anticipating the search to pick out a dog in due time, I began soliciting heavenly help. Reminiscent of inviting God into my husband-picking decision, I invited Him into this pet-picking decision. St. Francis of Assisi, the patron saint of animals, also became a daily confidant. I could not stop myself from going online to look at the faces of so many homeless dogs. Three months went by. Then I saw what seemed to be the perfect dog posted on an adoption website. "Zeus" was approximately six months old, living in a haven 50 miles away. His post included "HURRY" in bold, red letters. The lack of room and funding forced the shelter to euthanize unadopted animals within a short time. Zeus had already been housed at the facility for a month. His time was running out.

I could not get this puppy out of my mind. I showed Husband his online mug shot. Not only were the six months not up, but Husband proclaimed this dog as "butt ugly." I disagreed whole heartedly. In truth, he was a gangly creature with a head and paws too big for his body, but he needed a home.

Husband was scheduled to go out of town overnight on business. I took the opportunity to invite my then-teenage God-daughter, Molly, to keep me company. During her stay, I introduced her to Zeus' photo. We both thought it would be fun to hop in the car, drive the hour, and pay him a visit. We arrived at the shelter and asked to see him. The associate wildly motioned her arms and shook her head "no" as she whispered, "You don't want to see him. He's very hyper." That negative vibe was enough for me to walk away. Our previous dog had been a very anxious and sometimes aggressive dog. I didn't want the stress that goes with such a personality. Little Miss Molly sweetly whined, "Can't we see him anyway since we're here?" It was illogical to argue with her logic since we drove such a distance to see him. OK. The shelter lady whisked us off to the greeting room where we waited for her to bring the pup. He was so cute, so calm, and so polite. He didn't jump up on us in a frenzied display of any sort. My theory was that he became overly excited when a volunteer approached his pen with a leash in hand. He knew it was his chance to go outside. Because of short staffing, trips outdoors were only scheduled several times a day for potty time, not playtime. Zeus just couldn't wait to have a taste of freedom even if it was at the end of a rope.

The next evening, I shared with Husband all about the field trip with Molly and how wonderful this pup seemed. He listened and waited for me to finish gushing. His only comment was that we had an agreement. I went to bed with a burst bubble. Reflecting on my request to God that the next dog would be the best pet for both of us, prayers that night were practical. It had to be OUR dog, not mine. I didn't want to jump ahead and push the issue of this particular pet if it was not the time. I prayed, *Help me to be patient and wait. Please, Lord, if Zeus is the right dog, let my husband change his mind on his own. I won't say another word about it.* Early the next morning, Husband gave me my kiss goodbye and left for work. My day began as I made my way downstairs to make coffee. Before I reached the machine, I stopped in my tracks. A miracle waited for me on the kitchen counter in the form of a note. It read, "Wife, if you ***really*** want him, go get him. I'll warm up in time. XO." Hallelujah! Husband had changed his mind in his sleep, and I now had a permission slip to get "our" dog. I picked up the phone, called Molly and my sister, Josie, and off we went to pick up Zeus.

Any relationship requires love, work, energy, giving, and perseverance. We put the time into training and exercising our new puppy to keep him as a happy, healthy addition to our household. Zeus even had a stint at a local personal care home. He'd go to work periodically with Josie and shadow her for an eight-hour shift where she worked as a nursing assistant. He later worked greeting customers at a healthy pet food store where I was a part-time employee. Based on the joy Husband and I have found in him, I'd say Zeus was a "yes" answer to prayers. Another indication that he was a good choice is that Husband warmed up to him rather quickly. He's OUR dog for sure.

EYE-OPENER #4:   *Invite God into all things.*

My spiritual health was malnourished back when I was preparing to wed Mister. The advice received from Erin to invite God into marriage fell on deaf ears. Time would tick away before her wisdom came to light. The maturing process would someday have me trusting God enough to call Him into all aspects of life. Someday, I would become older and wiser to the point of believing that carrying God into everything makes anything better. I would reach the conclusion that inviting Him into all of our concerns unmistakably merges the earthly with the supernatural. This merger between Heaven and Earth always exists even when it is not acknowledged. However, when a sincere request is extended to God to bless and guide our undertakings, the union becomes discernible. Nothing tangible may change, but the grace is understood. This is trust. This is faith.

Someday, I would.

GOD EXPECTS ME
TO BE RECONCILED
WITH HIM

So we are ambassadors for Christ, since God is making His appeal through us; we entreat you on behalf of Christ, be reconciled to God. (2 CORINTHIANS 5:20)

Whoever, therefore, eats the bread or drinks the cup of the Lord in an unworthy manner will be answerable for the body and blood of the Lord. Examine yourselves, and only then eat of the bread and drink of the cup. (1 CORINTHIANS 11:27-28)

Once married, Husband and I continued to attend Mass together every Sunday. I received Jesus in the Eucharist each week, but I was unattached. It was nothing personal. Christ in the Eucharist was part of my childhood, which I held as truth, but the indifference with which I received Him was a shame. Neither had I been reconciled to God by asking for forgiveness of past indiscretions, which now included receiving the body and blood of the Lord unworthily.

My spouse escorted me back to the celebration of Mass, but I was in need of a reminder concerning God's grace through the sacrament of Confession a.k.a. Reconciliation. The reminder came through a guest priest who was celebrating the Sunday services one weekend. During his homily, he announced he would be speaking on the topic of reconciliation on an evening of the upcoming week. Presenting this fact alone did not attract my interest, but he still had another 14 minutes of sermon to go. As he continued, I was captivated by the message of his words explaining a sacrament first encountered in second grade. He invited all to come back during the week for more reflection and the opportunity to go to Confession. I went home and marked my calendar. Surprisingly, I kept the appointment. Over that day or two wait, grace kept my desire alive to go back to church on an "off day" and participate in this penitential celebration. While waiting in line for my turn, quiet tears rolled down my cheeks. Tears were becoming a familiar trademark when I sensed the presence of His love and mercy. Reconciliation is an outpouring of both.

As a note, I am compelled here to include a concept that I did not initially grasp. The Scripture in 1 Corinthians on the previous page cautions us against receiving our Lord unworthily. Receiving unworthily is not the same as feeling unworthy to receive our Lord in the Eucharist. As we grow in love for Christ, some of us struggle with a deep regret of past sins — that feeling of unworthiness — even after going to Confession, which keeps some away from the Eucharist. We are not made worthy on our own, but through the mercy of Christ. Jesus gave us His unfathomable love and mercy within the sacrament of Reconciliation. They are both also ever present through the Eucharist. If we have avoided serious sin since last confessing, we should not let this "feeling" hold us back from receiving the body and blood of our Lord. Instead, we do well to ask God to lead us to accept His profound love more fully within this precious, spiritual nourishment, and to run to Christ's embrace in the Eucharist.

EYE-OPENER #1:   *Awareness is the first step in moving forward.*

The priest's invitation moved me to receive the sacrament of Reconciliation that one evening, which played an important role in enhancing my relationship with God. It was a step toward Him, but it was with the stride of a child. Far from embracing Him on a natural-as-breathing level, my prayer time was still usually prompted by a need for something. Even so, I began wanting to go to Confession on a more regular basis with no need for a reminder.

The experience also triggered my adult thinking skills to kick in concerning this sacrament, and I wanted to know more. My vision and knowledge of Reconciliation was now in the process of moving beyond that of a second grader.

EYE-OPENER #2:   *Confessing out loud to a priest is healing for the mind, body, and spirit.*

Jesus said to them again, "Peace be with you. As the Father has sent me, so I send you." When he had said this, he breathed on them and said to them, "Receive the Holy Spirit. If you forgive the sins of any, they are forgiven them; if you retain the sins of any, they are retained." (JOHN 20:21-23)

There are Catholics and non-Catholics alike who don't get the point of going to a priest to confess sin. They see it as unnecessary because we can go straight to God to ask forgiveness. Yes, we can, and do, silently ask Him to forgive our trespasses. And He does. Yet, Christ made a point of ordaining His Apostles, His priests, with the Holy Spirit, and He gave them authority to forgive or retain "the sins of any." Priests continue in this capacity today.

Our Lord could read a person's heart and know if they were remorseful. Rarely do His ministers possess this same gift. We can reasonably conclude that, to carry out Christ's directive to forgive or retain, a priest must be privy to what sin was committed. It is, therefore, necessary for sins to be told aloud so he actually hears the apology. After hearing "the sins of any," the priest does not walk away. The repentant soul needs to hear that all is forgiven. This act of verbally acknowledging transgressions is for humanity's sake, not God's. Guilt and regret have a tendency to regurgitate if kept inside rather than being verbally expunged. God knows we need to purge for the benefit of both physical and spiritual health. The dose of humility and grace needed to do so in front of His priest is good for the soul. A huge burden lifts after this humbling, two-way exchange with the priest, who represents not only God, but also the whole Body of Christ, the Church community.

For a long time, I didn't get why I was taught that sin affects the entire Body of Christ. If I could get away with a questionable act without getting caught, how could it impact anyone else? Along the way of digging into my faith, I developed an understanding that the cause and effect on the entire community is real. The whole of the body is lacking if any of its members are not functioning properly. St. Paul preached about how individuals contribute to the support and growth of the Church as a whole:

> *The gifts he gave were that some would be apostles, some prophets, some evangelists, some pastors and teachers, to equip the saints for the work of ministry, for building up the body of Christ. But speaking the truth in love, we must grow up in every way into him who is the head, into Christ, from whom the whole body, joined and knit together by every ligament with which it is equipped, as each part is working properly, promotes the body's growth in building itself up in love.*
> *(EPHESIANS 4:11-12 AND 15-16)*

Sin puts the domino effect in motion. The damage wrongdoing does to a person may render that person unable to build others up in love until he or she has healed. Imagine if no one ever became lost in transgression. Instead of energy being spent doing wrong, it could be used reaching out, volunteering services, or praying for others. If everyone would live in harmony for the building up of another, there would be no victims of sin. Imagine the increase in stamina people would have to help others if they were spared the stress of physical or mental harm at the hands of someone else. Unfortunately, one person's detrimental action causes a reaction that prevents another from being the best he or she can be. Sin is self-centered behavior that has a negative impact on the whole community. Sin does not contribute to building others up and does not reflect the love of Christ. The sinner, the offended, and the community all suffer the loss of what might have been for the good.

GOD EXPECTS ME TO TALK TO HIM

Rejoice always, pray without ceasing, give thanks in all circumstances; for this is the will of God in Christ Jesus for you. (1 THESSALONIANS 5:16-18)

After failing to conceive after the second year of marriage, I took control of our efforts with a vain confidence. I faithfully recorded my temperature, bought a kit to monitor fruitfulness, counted cycle days in my sleep, and tapped Husband on the shoulder any time I felt the need to fertilize an egg. On top of these tools, I talked my man into some unconventional techniques that would assure us of pregnancy. He was a trooper in allowing me to take him wherever I must go. We visited an historic church where we endured the humbling, exhausting climb on our knees up the 28 steps of the "Scala Sancta" or Holy Stairs. The Holy Stairs are a representation of the stairs Jesus ascended to be judged in the praetorium of Pontius Pilate. As we traced our Savior's steps, my thoughts did not deliberate the sentence of suffering and crucifixion Christ received for the love of humanity. The impact of His sacrifice was lost on me. We made the climb because someone told me miracles happened at that church. The intent was solely to obtain the result of pregnancy. Next, Husband switched to boxer shorts because I read an article that briefs were too constricting. Peas were banned from our dinner table after I learned about a study in a distant land indicating these legumes could reduce fertility. The electric blanket was unplugged for fear it would fry my eggs or slow down Husband's contribution. While we entertained all of my conception voodoo, we also consulted a specialist, and I was placed on fertility drugs. None of these measures lived up to expectations, which moved me to the last trick in my bag. It was time to take God off the bottom shelf of my heart and dust Him off. I needed a favor.

OK, God, here I come.

EYE-OPENER #1:   *We crawl before we walk. We babble before we talk.*

I decided the best place to pray for a miracle would be in a church. An old, beautiful, Catholic church sat across the street from the downtown office building where I worked. This was such a convenience for someone in need of a miracle. The daily schedule for this particular church included a half hour "businessman's Mass" starting at noon. Immediately after Mass, the rosary was said and the Eucharist exposed for adoration of our Lord. My lunch hour fluctuated depending on deadlines being met, but if I began lunch at noon, I could attend Mass, say the rosary, pray for a baby, and make it back to my desk by 1:00 p.m. It was all very efficient.

Most people look both ways before crossing the street to avoid getting hit by a car. I'd look both ways to make sure nobody I knew would see me entering the church. Attending Mass daily might make me look like a religious fanatic, and I couldn't have that happen. I still had no inkling of what a personal, two-way relationship with God felt like. My motive for slipping into church was self-centered. I just wanted God to grant my wish, and then I could go back to spending my lunch hours eating lunch.

Mass in the middle of the week was a new experience. It impressed me deeply that people filling the pews on an "off day" were present because they wanted to be there. Saying the rosary was a familiar comfort because as a child I was very at home with the Blessed Mother Mary. As a miracle-seeking adult, I was a bit rusty at conversing with God. I knew the mother of God was an expert, so I asked her to talk to Him for me. The front, right side of the church displayed a beautiful statue and wall mural of the Blessed Mother holding the infant Jesus. This I deemed "Mary's side." Over on the front, left side, there stood a statue of Jesus and the Tabernacle where the Eucharist was housed. That must be His side. Whenever I entered the church, I sat in my comfort zone on Mary's side.

The difficult, unfamiliar zone was with this Jesus. I talked to "God." I still did not talk to the Son or the Holy Spirit. It was uncomfortable for me to even say the name Jesus. From my point of view, it was extremism to talk out loud about Him. I should know because my sister, Hannah, appeared to be over the top when conversing about Jesus. She had been getting to know God the Father, Son, and Holy Spirit for some time. Part of her spiritual growth included Bible studies, prayer groups, charismatic events, and healing services. She couldn't get enough of God and spouted off about the Trio as if they were changing her life. Mostly, I ignored Hannah's preaching and figured the phase she was going through would end in due time. I was afraid that if I took Jesus seriously, I would have to give up both my personality and my fun. When I got older I would look into Jesus, but not now. I was lukewarmness at its best.

I continued to go over to church frequently, if not daily, during the week to pray for a baby. Time rolled along. I was still plopping down on Mary's side, but my prayer time was becoming more peaceful and sincere than when I first began attending. As each month passed, my prayers focused on pregnancy, but a transition was taking place. I was getting comfortable with Jesus. Sitting on His mother's side of the church didn't mean I couldn't observe what was going on over on that other side. People would genuflect in the direction of Jesus' side before exiting. Some would stop by and kneel on the steps right in front of the Tabernacle. There came a day when I began to do the same before my departure.

God was patiently drawing me to the fullness of the Trinity over my many trips to church. During these early stages of pursuing my faith, I didn't ask others to help me figure out this unfolding relationship. Since I had dropped out of religious education right out of high school, I had no clue there was so much more to uncover. God did not hold it against me that I was only seeking my maternal path and not Him. He understood that I was sincere in my ignorance and genuine in my childish view of Him. As I approached, He would use whatever I brought to the table to have me grow up.

While I routinely occupied a seat in the pew, God's supernatural graces were kicking in to get me talking to His Son. Although oblivious to it, I received the powerful spiritual nourishment of the Eucharist almost daily. Eventually, I drifted over to Christ's side of the church for personal prayer after reciting the rosary. Lo and behold, I was talking to Jesus. Partial credit for this milestone may be attributed to Mary's intercession through her role as God's handmaiden. She initially presented Jesus physically to the world by giving birth to Him. From Heaven, she continues to serve God by interceding for people of today so they may also come to know Him. Frequently saying the rosary reintroduced me to her Son. Through the meditations within this prayer, I recounted Jesus' life and got to know Him better. Tracing my way through His life drew me to this Man whom I didn't know well at all.

Timidly, I began to kneel for a few moments before Jesus in the Tabernacle. My initial attempts at talking to Him were awkward. Heaven knows why, but when I first began addressing Him directly, my prayers were uttered in some sort of old, medieval English.

Hoping he would understand me, I spattered my sentences with words such as: thee, thou, thine, and thou art. Christ probably wanted to reach down and pinch my cheeks because His little girl was struggling to utter her first words to Him. After a few times, my visits became relaxed and down to earth. In due course, I couldn't wait until lunch to spend quiet time in a front pew before my Lord. I talked nonstop. He understood my language.

EYE-OPENER #2:   *Talking to God means listening too.*

Reminiscing about those years in the early nineties when I began going to daily Mass and adoration, I find that my spiritual spurts were most prominent over that time frame. My about-face was fast and furious, but immature. My prayer life may have started out awkwardly, but it progressed quickly. Still, unmindful of my one-sided prayerfulness, my growing relationship with God was missing a vital part of communication because I didn't stop to listen. On the other hand, that beginning was perfect because it was the only way I knew how to talk to Him at the time. A fervent prayer life does not develop overnight for most of us. With sincerity in the heart, it is OK to learn as you go. As with anything, invite your Father in Heaven to help deepen your bond of communication with Him.

The old saying "silence is golden" never dies. It takes discipline and true love to unplug the world to tune into God. We are at beck and call 24/7 due to the social networking technology of today. To get our attention, He may need to send a multi-media text announcing His appearance in a 90-second Super Bowl commercial asking everyone to shut down everything to hear Him in the silence.

People don't typically hear a big, manly, bellowing voice of God talking to them the way the movies portray hearing His voice. It is difficult to perceive anything the Lord might be trying to get across if we never truly stop to listen. It is in silence that He is able to touch our hearts and minds one-on-one. For the love of God, we need to quiet down to be able to discern the Spirit's guidance.

EYE-OPENER #3:   *Prayer life matures as our relationship with God matures and vice versa.*

Communication and spending time together are keys to any lasting relationship. This applies just as surely to a relationship with our Father in Heaven. Increasing prayer and personal time fuels the furnace with faith, hope, and love.

A most perfect example of the need for talking to God is given to us by Christ, who is of both human and divine natures. Because of His divine nature, He had no need to ask for help in anything, but He constantly went to God the Father in prayer. Scripture stories are chock full of Jesus praying. He not only preached prayer, He practiced it. You name it, He prayed for it. He prayed for others; He prayed for Himself; He prayed before performing miracles; He prayed to thank God; He prayed to do the Father's will. Christ prayed all for the glory of God. The Father responded with love and filled Him with the power and peace of the Spirit. Jesus' prayers were for our sake to demonstrate how to get through life in the flesh and remain holy. The bottom line is that He taught us to talk to God about everything. If we choose to live Christ's example, we will be building up our relationship with the Father. The Father responds to us in the same way He responded to the Son, that is, with His love, grace, and the power of the Spirit. He acts with perfect, fatherly love with what He knows is best for us.

My initial uncomfortable moments of talking to God are gone. Two decades later, it is notable that my prayer life has been enhanced by the maturing process that time affords. My faith remains strong, and I find myself praying constantly during the day like a child with an invisible friend. I'm praying on the run, in the car, while I'm working, or while grocery shopping. Praying constantly is a good thing as it mimics Christ's example. It becomes natural. I'm happy that God is so much on my mind, but it's also natural to get side-tracked or interrupted. I try hard to allow myself the quiet, intimate setting that lends itself to getting lost in the embrace of God's inner whisperings. Examples are when I sit before the Tabernacle, spend time in adoration, read spiritually-inspiring literature, or whole-heartedly set out with my dog on the wooded trails for quiet talking with the Lord. Within these peaceful settings, I anticipate that He will respond through the Spirit within my soul. It is when I seek these moments of tremendous bonding with God that I am most graced with His discernible presence. Constant praying on the run is an awesome method of communicating with Him, but it is a different kind of prayer than carving out time to be with the Lord in silence. We need both.

Faith at any level needs to be nourished with prayer. Sometimes my devotion suffers like my house plants when I forget to water them until the leaves curl under. Those sorry looking leaves remind me that the health of my plants has been neglected. Miraculously, within hours of tending to their necessities, the foliage looks vibrant again. Every now and again, my faith feels like it's curling a bit around the edges. Most likely, I can trace it to not giving myself the nourishment of spending time with God – just the two of us. As soon as I realize I'm curling under, I ask God for the nourishment to flourish again, and for the discipline to make sure my spiritual needs are not neglected. At times I feel His presence and it waters me. At times I don't, but I trust He is listening. He is good at that.

GOD EXPECTS ME TO LEARN FROM OTHERS — WITH HIS GUIDANCE

In the third year of his reign he sent his officials ... to teach in the cities of Judah ... and with these Levites, the priests Elishama and Jehoram. They taught in Judah, having the book of the law of the Lord with them; they went around through all the cities of Judah and taught among the people. (2 CHRONICLES 17:7-9)

For learning about wisdom and instruction, for understanding words of insight, for gaining instruction in wise dealing, righteousness, justice, and equity; to teach shrewdness to the simple, knowledge and prudence to the young — let the wise also hear and gain in learning, and the discerning acquire skill, to understand a proverb and a figure, the words of the wise and their riddles. The fear of the Lord is the beginning of knowledge; fools despise wisdom and instruction. (PROVERBS 1:2-7)

Those self-centered visits to church to pray for pregnancy overlapped with Hannah's repeated invitations to attend the charismatic prayer sessions. Although I did not initially pay much attention to her spiritual witness, other family members did. Mom, Dad, and some of my sisters accepted her invitation to join this small prayer group at our home parish. I begged her pardon, but I couldn't possibly make it because the church group met every Friday evening, the same night that my own group gathered at a local pub. Husband and I would stay downtown after work socializing with friends. Friday was our date night. We had a blast!

Hannah would periodically catch me on a visit home and update me on her love for God, Jesus, and what the Holy Spirit was doing these days. After repeatedly hearing about these wonderful prayer sessions from my loved ones, I was beginning to wear down with curiosity. The clincher came when I was told that the group prayed for each other. They prayed for healings, both spiritual and physical. Hmmmmmm. There was no sense wasting any more time. I arranged to meet up with the group so they would pray for a physical healing resulting in pregnancy. Husband was fine with me getting pregnant via prayer since it didn't involve any diet restrictions or wardrobe changes on his part.

Arriving at my first meeting, I entered the room and slid into a back row, corner chair. I didn't want to bother anybody nor did I want to talk. It was a very disconcerting evening. People were praying out loud to the Father God, to Jesus, and to the Holy Spirit as if it were normal. These people held their arms into the air while praying and singing praises. Someone was even shaking a tambourine. Just about everyone except me was swaying and dancing in place. They had a blast!

On that Friday, I did not participate. During the entire prayer and praise segment, I was quietly sobbing in my own little corner in my own little chair. Part of me was crying because I felt I didn't belong. Part of me was crying because I recognized God. He was within these people who unabashedly loved Him. These men and women appeared to be holy, which, in those days, was a condition I considered to be outside of my reach. After the meeting was over, I did not stay to socialize. I said goodbye to my family and gave a quick wave to the crowd. On my way out, these strange people invited me to come back.

For some reason I wanted to go back. From the moment I stepped into the room that evening, I was welcomed and not judged. No one seemed to mind that I hid in the back not saying a word, and no one pushed or pried. Before giving this event another shot, I needed to weigh the dilemma of disappointing Husband by skipping happy hour to attend the prayer group. Breaking our date one or two Fridays in a month wouldn't seem too much – would it? One could say I was doing it for "us" since we both wanted a baby. Attendance once a month turned into weekly because I fell into enjoying the prayer and praise goings-on.

Never would I become comfortable swaying my hands in the air. I did, however, become less awkward at thanking God for everything and anything that is, was, and will be, and asking for anything and everything for my personal needs. That wasn't much at the time. A baby would be perfect. Although my "gimme, gimme, gimme" prayer style evolved to one of hope, I was still unaware of how narrow minded my motives remained.

While I was fixated on getting my miracle, the prayer group simultaneously reintroduced me to the Bible. I use the word "reintroduced" because I was already hearing Scripture at every Mass attended. Along with hearing two or three readings and a Psalm, the majority of the priest's words, and the people's responses, quoted or paraphrased the Bible in terms of prayer, praise, worship, or thanksgiving. Even though I had not yet picked up the habit of reading the Bible on my own, it is no wonder that much of what I was hearing on Fridays sounded so familiar.

EYE OPENER #1:   *In the beginning ... there were bloopers.*

Sharing Scripture was the most interesting portion of the prayer group format for me. We didn't study Scripture book by book, but rather discussed inspirations and quotes at random. These knowledgeable, faithful people were telling me that God speaks to us through Scripture. This was not good information for an immature Christian because I was able to pick and choose which verses suited my fancy. Each week, I mostly looked forward to the healing prayers and the Bible messages meant just for me. The Bible talked about old women, like Sarah and Elizabeth, becoming pregnant through miracles. One story led me to announce that I was going to get pregnant immediately because I finished reading that the prophet Elisha told a Shunammite woman that she would have a son in the spring (2 Kings 4:8-17), and she did so right on schedule. An elderly gentleman in the group would encourage me to have faith that God would give me my heart's desire. He would often relay messages from the Bible that kept my hope alive as I counted my cycles away each month. Fridays couldn't come quickly enough so that I could find out if my messenger had anything new for me that week. If he wasn't at the meeting, I was distraught and not at all into praying or praising. God must have been shaking His head as he looked down to see my confusion in pursuing messages instead of time with Him. Forgive me, Lord, I knew not what I was doing.

My high points were cloaked in the anticipation of getting pregnant. My low points stemmed from an obsession with Satan. Not only did our group talk about God's love, goodness, and miracles, we discussed Satan's totally opposite nature and activities. The leaders taught songs and prayers intended to keep the Devil at bay. I was shown a cute little routine that some of the attendees followed each morning. It involved mimicking a scene from Scripture depicting getting dressed with the armor of God (Eph 6:13-17). From my naïve viewpoint, I grew to believe that I must be proactive to keep Satan from possessing me both physically and spiritually. I did not get into the habit of the dressing motions, but I would routinely blast Satan with the name of Jesus to keep him running scared.

Unfortunately, I began doing this constantly throughout each day worried that if I didn't, I would be over taken. I would wake up at night thinking the fiend was standing at the foot of the bed waiting for his chance to steal my soul. My dramatic fear of being possessed was pitiful and not at all the way God wants us to go about life. He wants us to revel in joy and peace with Him by our side. I don't remember who said it, but I got my peace back after hearing about a quote referring to Satan, which asked, "Why would you want to talk to that fellow anyway?" From that day forward, talking to God and staying focused on Him keeps my home-made fears away and allows me to walk with Him in peace.

The Friday night sessions were pulling me in God's direction, and I continued to learn about Him. Tiny step by tiny step, He was using my one-sided communication skills, and my hope of conceiving, to teach me. It was later, not sooner, when I came to understand that my initial enthusiasm for the prayer group activities was misplaced and immature. It is not a good idea to push the Lord aside for a "prophet." Nor would I recommend canceling a standing date with a spouse to attend a prayer group without further consideration of everything involved. As a loving wife to my husband, I have a duty and a vocation to him. While in pursuit of spiritual growth, I had to learn to balance my vocation to my husband and my vocation to my God. With God as the lifeblood, the two should be intertwined, but I treated them as separate worlds.

Husband is a very rare breed of man. He was always able to read into my various stages, emotions, and pursuits. He saw them as lessons in personal development, and recognized that I was not pushing him away in favor of more interesting interests. Intuitively, he knew that I would eventually obtain balance. He may not have voiced the sentiment, but he understood that God draws good from everything, and good things come to those who wait. My spouse patiently waited for me to come back down to Earth and use the heavenly things I learned in a more productive, mature manner.

I have to laugh at a few of my naive, adolescent attempts at following my faith during those phases of stumbling into maturity. My original struggles of talking "baby talk" to Jesus were long gone, but I still had episodes of learning the hard way while trying to live my studies. There was the day I returned a new vacuum cleaner in exchange for a different brand. Prior to the purchase, I had researched different manufacturers to get consumer ratings on certain models of sweepers. The "Dirt Devil" rated well. I bought it, but couldn't bring myself to use it because it honored the Devil's name. Back it went. Today I would enjoy that the adjective "dirt" would put the dirtbag in his place. There was also that time I announced with confidence that I would immediately become pregnant after reading the Scripture story about a miraculous pregnancy. I had no such miracle.

EYE OPENER #2:   *Learn to prayerfully ponder God's view on the matter.*

This period in my relationship with God could be considered the "New Christian Syndrome." This stage of growing up in Him is a common phenomenon, which involves ups and downs of emotions, embarrassments, and stories with much ado. I was so excited about my spiritual discoveries that I wanted to gush to anyone that would listen. Gushing can push people away in a hurry because an immature, discovering Christian can be a baby trying to run before learning to walk. I was progressing, but didn't necessarily have mature, knowledgeable information to share with others. Also, the way in which I continued to use God as a means to my end – a miracle baby – contributed to holding me back from understanding the deepness of His Word.

Some errors in judgment may have been avoided had I followed Jesus' mother's example. In Scripture, we read of Mary receiving words of wisdom from God's messengers. She is described as pondering all these things in her heart. She thinks about them, prays about them, and thinks about them some more. While processing information, I'm sure Mary sought direction from Heaven to understand more about what she was given. In my early days of befriending God, I was intent on my own course and did not search my heart for His. It's as if I forgot He was a part of my religious experience. When a Scripture "spoke to me," or the TV evangelist talked about an infertile couple conceiving, or I received "a word" from a wiser-than-me messenger, I reacted impulsively instead of first asking God for guidance, wisdom, and understanding from His viewpoint. I've since learned to pray and ponder before twisting every word into a "sign" in my favor.

GOD EXPECTS ME TO GROW IN WISDOM AND KNOWLEDGE

Take my instruction instead of silver, and knowledge rather than choice gold; for wisdom is better than jewels, and all that you may desire cannot compare with her. (PROVERBS 8:10-11)

If any of you is lacking in wisdom, ask God, who gives to all generously and ungrudgingly, and it will be given you. But ask in faith, never doubting, for the one who doubts is like a wave of the sea, driven and tossed by the wind, for the doubter, being double minded and unstable in every way, must not expect to receive anything from the Lord. (JAMES 1:5-8)

Today's trend is to quit learning about God immediately after receiving the sacrament of Confirmation. This tendency to refrain from religious classes takes place around the tender age of 13. Parents stand their ground if a child entertains dropping out of high school. They find it difficult to comply if their young graduate hesitates to attend college or trade school. Yet we have become so comfortable letting our children stagnate in knowledge about the most important Entity of life. Perhaps this is because there exists a cycle of religious education dropouts over several generations. This creates parents who have not matured beyond teenagers when it comes to a relationship with God. Religious immaturity is passed along to sons and daughters. It may not be a lack of concern, but the lack of higher religious instruction in adults that prevents passing on Godly information to children. With this lack of knowledge, we breed a lack of wisdom. Our children are prone to being driven and tossed about by the wind as they become of the world and detached from the little they know of the Father, Son, and Holy Spirit.

When we stop seeking spiritual growth, we are in danger of being blind to graces that pull us toward, and keep us steeped in, divine favor and wisdom.

EYE OPENER #1:   *God wants us to have the faith of a child, not remain as naïve as a child.*

Some would argue that it is not necessary to pursue religious education because Scripture encourages us to become like children in humility, faith, and trust:

> *At that time the disciples came to Jesus and asked, "Who is the greatest in the kingdom of heaven?" He called a child, whom he put among them, and said, "Truly I tell you, unless you change and become like children, you will never enter the kingdom of heaven. Whoever becomes humble like this child is the greatest in the kingdom of heaven. Whoever welcomes one such child in my name welcomes me." (MATTHEW 18:1-5)*

Scripture also makes no bones about the necessity of growing in knowledge and understanding of our faith:

> *About this we have much to say that is hard to explain, for you have become dull in understanding. For though by this time you ought to be teachers, you need someone to teach you again the basic elements of the oracles of God. You need milk, not solid food; for everyone who lives on milk, being still an infant, is unskilled in the word of righteousness. But solid food*

is for the mature, for those whose faculties have been trained by practice to distinguish good and evil. (HEBREWS 5:11-14)

Therefore, let us go on toward perfection, leaving behind the basic teaching about Christ and not laying again the foundation. (HEBREWS 6:1)

Healthy people do not remain children forever in body, mind, or spirit. Although we will never totally understand the ways of God, He expects us to gain knowledge of Him through Scripture and instruction just as we seek further education to reach other personal goals.

Yes, we should have the faith of a youngster when it comes to trusting unconditionally that we can depend on God always. Yet, we must grow up to be mature teachers of that faith. To do so responsibly requires learning the ins and outs of our religious convictions in order to answer children as they grow to pose questions. As God blesses us with greater wisdom and understanding of all He expects, we become better equipped to discern good from evil and better mentors to those we teach. At the same time, it becomes more natural to possess the faith of a child in the areas of trusting God, depending on Him, and being joyfully obedient to Him.

EYE OPENER #2:   *We have a responsibility to pursue knowledge of God and grow in faith.*

A couple years after I began participating in the prayer group, it disbanded. I had matured enough to pursue Scripture study on my own, and now took time daily to feed this spiritual hunger. My intent was to read the Bible from beginning to end instead of concentrating on a few choice passages. This included frustration because I began with the Old Testament without any working knowledge of the New. The Old Testament was especially odd. How could God put up with all the awful things being done by a populace that supposedly loved Him? Why did He let it happen? Amazingly, my questions concerning some deplorable behavior by those ancient people were the same questions I once yelled at Him about for the conduct of modern inhabitants. Nothing is ever new. It's old in a new way. As proven through the test of time, our Father loves His children despite the tendency to stray. Thank God He encourages us through love, mercy, and forgiveness to try and try again as we battle to get things right.

My prayer time, thinking time, and understanding mushroomed amidst the peace and quiet of sitting alone with God. I studied Scripture at every opportunity that came about. Soon, I opted to skip ahead of the Old Testament and move onto the New. Footnotes were invisible at first, but as I progressed, they intrigued me and became a vital learning tool. I purchased Bible study guides to help me understand the significance of text in the period of time it was written and God's messages within. As reading the Bible became my steady pastime, I grew out of the toddler stage into a young adult viewpoint of God. Most nights after Husband fell asleep, I quietly turned the light back on and opened the Bible. Habitually taking notes into the wee hours of the morning, I discovered answers to many WHYs. All along the way, I was graced with God's guidance in learning things that I did not set out to learn.

Beside Scripture, my reading habits took a turn toward other spiritually related literature. Books were extremely helpful in allowing me to digest the Old Testament. I came to understand the connection between the Old and the New Testaments, and what they both had to do with me. The more I uncovered about Jesus through Scripture, the more I yearned to get closer to Him. The Old Testament was like a huge, heavy, iron door that could not be muscled open. The New Testament made the door easier to enter. They meld together. Studying one without the other is kin to unwrapping a present, but, in all the excitement, a second gift is overlooked and left lying at the bottom of the same box.

This enthusiasm for Scripture was a grace that took me deeper into my relationship with God. His gifts of wisdom and knowledge allowed the film of self-centeredness that initially trademarked my prayers to peel away. Although Husband and I still hoped for a child, it was now love for God in union with His love for me that was moving me to further grow in Him.

GOD EXPECTS ME TO ASK HIM TO LEAD ME THROUGH THE FOG

But above all pray to the Most High that he may direct your way in truth. (SIRACH 37:15)

When I lived as a lapsed Catholic, I was not compelled to speak of religious beliefs. My silence kept me safe from others trying to "save" me. In some ways, this was easier than living an open faith. By the middle of the nineties, my spiritual zeal was apparent and had me sharing the joy of knowing God better. As I opened myself up to others, I began running into countering points of view, criticism, and even an air of anger at the notion of Catholicism. Protestant acquaintances seemed to know their stuff when it came to Scripture, and they introduced me to opposing interpretations that I could not yet respond to with confidence. A fog set in surrounding what I had come to understand about particular Scriptures, Christ's teachings, and the Church. I was introduced to beliefs and perspectives that protested what I held as solid gold Truth. If I was barking up the wrong tree, I wanted to find the right tree. I needed to clear my head of conflicting information against certain religious convictions I was taught as a child. The first thing I did before opening a book, beginning a bout of research, or studying was to pray to the Most High that He may direct my way in Truth as He meant it to be for everyone, everywhere. My heart was open to wherever God would lead.

Some of the subjects that often stir up confusion are addressed in the remainder of this chapter. The information shared goes a bit beyond the simple descriptions given to children and would most likely be learned only if a person pursues some adult studies. These are "meaty" topics, and I present them in order to connect-the-dots between the WHAT and the WHY of these beliefs. These are the topics that were not clear to me until I took it upon myself to find out more, usually because I was asked a question I could not answer. My hope is that by sharing my passion for this information, more of us will be able to answer others when they ask us why.

EYE-OPENER #1:   *It is perfectly OK to honor Mary, the mother of Jesus, the ideal Christian model.*

Rolling further into the nineties, still feeding my desire to study the Bible and other spiritual literature, I added a Christian radio station as my companion in the car. One talk show in particular caught my interest, but this source of information brought with it both education and confusion. Two male hosts invited people to call the show with Bible questions, and they would reply with a great deal of wisdom and confidence. Their answers were sometimes quite the opposite of what I recollected. One day as I listened, these gentlemen announced a shocking discrepancy that flattened my own beliefs. The topic was Mary, the mother of Jesus. These radio men agreed that Mary was certainly chosen by God to be the mother of Jesus. However, they disagreed she deserved the honor bestowed on her by Catholics. They believed that Catholics' hearts were in the right place, but they broadcasted that members of that Church participated in idol worship of a woman. Furthermore, the two stated that the visions of her held as being from God were actually coming through Satan. Gasp! I was devastated. They declared that I was worshipping a false idol and breaking the very first commandment. God help me. I quit talking to the mother of Jesus.

In the past, my reaction to opposition was to automatically abandon my own thinking and adopt someone else's. For a couple of months, I repeated that pattern, but I missed the Blessed Mother. I certainly didn't think of her as a god. It just did not sit right with me to kick her out of my life. I paid attention to that still, small voice deep within me. Instead of walking away from this Catholic fidelity without both sides of the story, I decided to check things out. The first thing I did was buy the Catechism of the Catholic Church to accompany me on this quest. My search for information was prior to having home access to the Internet and search engines. My methods were old fashioned by today's standards, but the world of books put the world of Mary at my fingertips.

Shortly after beginning my investigation about Mary's place in my life, Scripture and the wisdom of the Church rang clear in my heart. I ran back to my spiritual mother and adopted the Church's judgment that she is the perfect role model. She was the first person to accept Christ into her life when she consented to be His mother. With this "yes" to God's design, she became the first Christian. Mary gave herself totally to God and trusted Him completely as He helped her pioneer living the Christian life. This holy woman's example is certainly worth imitating.

Confirming Church dogma on Mary, I now wanted to know the WHY behind what I knew about her. This trait of mine, this desire for detail, which prompts me to ask exhaustive questions, drives my husband mad. Fortunately for him, when I began my rampage for spiritual information, I conducted a silent inquisition. Questions were on my mind, but I was still in the phase of not asking advice from others, but sought answers in the written word. Not everyone has this same need for intricacies for their religious convictions. For me, it is the flowing, non-stop, dot connecting between the Old and New that sends my heart aflutter. I want the gory particulars that link me to each verse explored.

Mary is explicitly introduced in Scripture through Luke's Gospel. The following passages from Luke reveal much about her as the first Christian:

> *In the sixth month the angel Gabriel was sent by God to a town in Galilee called Nazareth, to a virgin engaged to a man whose name was Joseph, of the house of David. The virgin's name was Mary. And he came to her and said, "Greetings, favored one! The Lord is with you." But she was much perplexed by his words and pondered what sort of greeting this might be. The angel said to her, "Do not be afraid, Mary, for you have found favor with God. And now, you will conceive in your womb and bear a son, and you will name him Jesus. Mary said to the angel, "How can this be, since I am a virgin?" The angel said to her, "The Holy Spirit will come upon you, and the power of the Most High will overshadow you; therefore the child to be born will be called holy; he will be called Son of God. And now, your relative Elizabeth in her old age has also conceived a son; and this is the sixth month for her who was said to be barren. For nothing will be impossible with God." Then Mary said, "Here am I, the servant of the Lord; let it be with me according to your word." (LUKE 1:26-31, 34-38)*

After the angel announced that God wanted Mary to be the mother of His Son, she responded with a strong example of faith. She agreed to His plan despite the fact that she didn't know what the future held.

There Mary stood before God the Father's angel, and he introduced her to the other two members of the Trinity: the Son and the

Holy Spirit. She was holy, full of grace, and had a love for God so overwhelming that it outweighed any fear of the unknown. Then, to boot, after being told her elderly relative Elizabeth was pregnant, Mary rode off to see her. Telecommunications didn't exist that would allow her to ask Elizabeth from afar if what the angel proclaimed was true. Mary fervently believed that nothing was impossible with God. With her faith in tow, she set off on a difficult journey to serve her kinswoman in a time of need and to share the wonder of God.

My pursuit of "why" is a natural quirk. Finding answers to my questions allows me to go deeper and more fully into my covenant with the Almighty. It was very soothing for me to ponder the fact that before Mary gave her consent, "Let it be with me according to your word," she asked a question. At first, the young lady was a bit confused as an angel told her she was to become pregnant. Mary asked an honest question, "How can this be?" Understanding how women become pregnant and knowing she was not, she sincerely and respectfully asked the angel for clarification. Gabriel explained to her the miracle of God's intent, and her tremendous faith allowed her to embrace the Lord's will wholeheartedly. Asking questions is a healthy response to His call when done so with a sincere heart.

Reading further on in the story, Elizabeth excitedly says to Mary, "Blessed are you among women" and calls her "the mother of my Lord":

And Elizabeth was filled with the Holy Spirit and exclaimed with a loud cry, "Blessed are you among women, and blessed is the fruit of your womb. And why has this happened to me, that the mother of my Lord comes to me?" (LUKE 1:41-43)

It was the Holy Spirit who transferred this knowledge about Mary to Elizabeth. Mary is, therefore, without a doubt, a very blessed mother. She is the mother of our Lord, Jesus, our God. That is most certainly a position worthy of honor.

Also in Luke, we read "Mary's Song" where she praises God for all He has done and will do. Within her song of praise, we read:

And Mary said, "My soul magnifies the Lord, and my spirit rejoices in God my Savior, for he has looked with favor on the lowliness of his servant. Surely, from now on all generations will call me blessed." (LUKE 1:46-48)

"All generations" includes us. It was very moving to learn that every time I call Mary the "Blessed Mother," I take part in biblical prophecy.

Mary is also seen as a great intercessor in taking our needs before her Son. In Scripture, she takes this intercessory role at the wedding in Cana. When the wine ran out during the celebration, Mary acted as mediator for the family by bringing the embarrassing situation to her Son's attention. She did not tell Jesus what to do, but trusted that whatever He decided would be for the best. Instead, she gave the staff profound advice that we would also be wise to heed:

His mother said to the servants, "Do whatever he tells you." (JOHN 2:5)

The servants obeyed. It followed that Jesus performed his first public miracle by turning water into wine to meet the needs of the wedding hosts and then some. Mary's intervention at Cana points us once again to that two-way street. In a relationship with the Lord we expect Him to look after our needs. He expects us to "do whatever He tells you."

Mary acted on behalf of the hosts even though it was not a matter of life and death. Running out of wine may not be the worst thing that could happen, but it was of urgent concern for the parties involved. Many times I have asked the Blessed Mother to talk to her Son for me on issues that may seem insignificant to someone else. Even so, I trust she understands they are important to me, and that she will assist according to God's will.

As I became more prayerfully involved in meditating upon the rosary, there were two mysteries that were not clear in my head as to why I grew up believing them. The teachings, or the WHATs, of these mysteries included:

1. Mary was assumed both body and soul into Heaven.
2. She is Queen of Heaven.

Both teachings about Jesus' mother intertwine and are rooted in Scripture with most of the explicit information about Mary found in the Gospel of Luke. I enjoyed reading Luke, but I had to dig further. The Catechism was a tremendous help in explaining our relationship, and Church history, surrounding our spiritual Mother, but it did not provide the detail I craved with respect to these specific teachings. I branched out and bought books about the Mother of God. Some provided information that helped and some did not. Resources eventually led back to Scripture in the Book of Revelations. The Church's discernment of Mary's bodily appearance in Heaven, both as a queen with a crown and as the mother of Jesus, correlates to Scripture as described by John the Evangelist in his vision of the heavens opening up:

A great portent appeared in heaven: a woman clothed with the sun, with the moon under her feet, and on her head a crown of twelve stars. She was pregnant and was crying out in birth pangs, in the agony of giving birth. Then another portent appeared in heaven: a great red dragon, with seven heads and ten horns, and seven diadems on his heads. His tail swept down a third of the stars of heaven and threw them to the earth. Then the dragon stood before the woman who was about to bear a child, so that he might devour her child as soon as it was born. And she gave birth to a son, a male child, who is to rule all the nations with a rod of iron. But her child was snatched away and taken to God and to his throne; and the woman fled into the wilderness, where she has a place prepared by God. (REVELATIONS 12:1-6)

The Church explains that the pregnant woman in Revelations represents both Mary and the Church. Both participate in God's plan of redemption through Jesus, the Messiah. I will not go into further explanation, but I do highly recommend pursuing the fascinating Biblical background and Church teaching concerning our Blessed Mother Mary.

In all that I came to understand about God's chosen servant Mary, I can most surely picture our risen Lord at His holy mother's side as her earthly duties ended. I can vividly imagine Him lifting her gently and lovingly into His arms to carry her home.

EYE-OPENER #2:   *It is perfectly OK to talk to dead saints, friends, and relatives through the "communion of saints."*

Jesus said to them, … "And as for the dead being raised, have you not read in the book of Moses, in the story about the bush, how God said to him, 'I am the God of Abraham, the God of Isaac, and the God of Jacob'? He is God not of the dead, but of the living." (MARK 12:24-27)

Another issue that causes confusion is why some of us earthlings talk to Mary, other saints, and relatives that have already gone to meet our Maker. Those who do not talk to our heavenly brothers and sisters offer the explanation that they pray straight to Jesus. On the other hand, I am one of those who make it a habit to talk to dead saints. At the same time, I am in agreement that it is well and good to talk directly to Jesus. We should talk to Him often. God instructs us to keep in touch with Him — to pray — constantly. This is for our sake, not His. Prayer takes us deeper into a relationship with Him just as communicating with another person helps develop that relationship. We talk to God knowing full well that He does not need those prayers in order to get things done. He also encourages us to pray for one another. Following instructions, the family of God prays for one another.

This family encompasses not only God's children living on Earth, but also those who have died. His physically-deceased people are actually still living because He promises eternal life to those who love and believe in Him. Thus "He is God not of the dead, but of the living." This inclusion in His living family is what makes up the "communion of saints." As common as it is for people to ask others to pray for their intentions, many among us request prayer help from deceased members of God's family. Just as we are bound to obey the commandments, the dearly departed are bound to "love God above all else and love thy neighbor." Praying for one's neighbor is an act of love. It is a service. It is compassion. That's what the faithful do in communion. We pray. Those having gone before us do so more perfectly now and without the distractions of earthly things. They are able to dedicate themselves to the worship of God and to loving others.

I have my own favorite saints who I go to for assistance. I'm not drawn to talk to Abraham, Isaac, or Jacob. Instead, I'm inclined to ask help from deceased individuals who I connect to more person-ally. A few examples include Joan of Arc, who is my confirmation saint, Pope John Paul II, the Blessed Mother, my grandmothers, my Dad, and other relatives and friends who have died. In death, all of these people remain part of God's family. Therefore, they are my family, too. They are souls willing and able to intercede for me before God. I talk to them often.

My husband has a go-to saint stemming from his knack for carpentry. Out of his love for woodworking, Husband has formed a bond with St. Joseph, the carpenter. Anytime my spouse has an urge to begin a new project or knock down this or that to build something else, he talks to St. Joseph looking for inspiration.

With tongue in cheek, I tell about a "communion of saints" moment with Pope John Paul II after his death in 2005. In this texting age he is known as JP2. Although I didn't pay much attention to him until I became interested in my religious roots, I grew up during his pontificate. As I grew in my faith, my heart grew very fond of this man. Upon his death, I began asking for his intercession about different things on a fairly regular basis. I had in my possession a CD which included inspirational comments and snippets by John Paul II. My favorite piece on that CD was the Pope singing "The Our Father" in Latin. His rendition was so cute in such a beautiful way. I found myself listening to the recording in my car player everywhere I went. Not only did I listen, but my voice joined his in praying the Lord's Prayer in harmony via technology. The volume would be blasting so I could hear his voice over my own. One day, I was singing my little heart out along with the Pope when my cell phone rang. I could not hear the ring tone. I did not respond, but my phone answered automatically allowing hands-free use of it. Amidst the musical joy in the car, I was deaf to my husband's "hello" on the other end. Over our ritual, pre-dinner coffee that evening, Husband mentioned he tried calling, but he figured I was busy since the Pope answered. Knowing my feelings for JP2, this did not surprise him, but he was a bit concerned about the "roaming" charges associated with such a long-distance connection.

EYE-OPENER #3: *Christ founded His Church, elected leadership to preserve His teachings, and set the stage for all generations to hear His Truth.*

The controversy over Mary led me to discover the wisdom and guidance of the Catholic Church. As I was being challenged more often to sort through the mixed bag of information and opinions on particular topics, it became a habit to pick up the Catechism to read the WHYs, which explained the WHATs of doctrine in relation to Scripture. The Church became the mother I could run to when I needed to clarify a concept, and her Catechism became my tried and true resource on the teachings of Christ. Although I might compare the Catechism to an encyclopedia used to obtain background and explanation, I found myself reading it as an unfolding drama series.

Seeking the Church's guidance through the Catechism had a side effect. While I gained knowledge about Scripture in relation to my beliefs, I also gained an understanding that my spiritual relationship with God was destined to go deeper than I had yet discovered. Researching the foundation I grew up on became a joy as it drew me further into my bond with our Lord.

I found myself turning to the Church for answers even before I had any appreciation for the Biblical basis behind the authoritative role assigned by Christ to the Church.

In my early days of shining with the joy of Christ, a co-worker made a comment about how Catholics worship the Pope. I tried explaining that we do not worship him, but we do have a great deal of respect and love for him as God's representative on Earth, and we show it. The conversation set me in motion to find the WHY regarding the role of the Pope as the leader of Christ's Church. Resources pointed to Scripture, which laid out the role of the Pope within the Church in the mission to protect the fullness of God's Word, including:

> *Now when Jesus came into the district of Caesarea Philippi, he asked his disciples, "Who do people say that the Son of Man is?" And they said, "Some say John the Baptist, but others Elijah, and still others Jeremiah or one of the prophets." He said to them, "But who do you say that I am?" Simon Peter answered, "You are the Messiah, the Son of the living God." And Jesus answered him, "Blessed are you, Simon son of Jonah! For flesh and blood has not revealed this to you, but my Father in heaven. And I tell you, you are Peter, and on this rock I will build my church, and the gates of Hades will not prevail against it. I will give you the keys of the kingdom of heaven, and whatever you bind on earth will be bound in heaven, and whatever you loose on earth will be loosed in heaven." (MATTHEW 16:13-19)*

Let's take a sentence or two at a time from the above verses and look at the relevancy to the Church today:

1. *He asked His disciples, "Who do people say that the Son of Man is?" And they said, "Some say John the Baptist, but others Elijah, and still others Jeremiah or one of the prophets."*

The differing answers to Jesus' first question indicate that the average follower thought of Jesus as a holy, great man, but did not realize the Son of God stood among them. For many today, this lack of recognition of Jesus as God's promised Savior remains.

2. *He said to them, "But who do you say that I am?" Simon Peter answered, "You are the Messiah, the Son of the living God."*

Peter is the disciple who came up with the right answer to Jesus' second question. He correctly identified Jesus as the Son of God, the Savior.

3. *And Jesus answered Him, "Blessed are you, Simon son of Jonah! For flesh and blood has not revealed this to you, but my Father in heaven."*

Jesus excitedly told Simon that he is blessed because he spoke the Truth that Jesus is the Messiah. The Lord explained that Simon did not come up with this Truth on his own. The Apostle was given this infallible knowledge supernaturally through the Father in Heaven.

4. *And I tell you, you are Peter, and on this rock I will build my church, and the gates of Hades will not prevail against it.*

The Father revealed a surefire Truth to Simon, which signaled Jesus to assign him to lead His Church. Jesus called Simon by a new name, Peter, which means "rock." In preparation for His death, Jesus assigned Peter as the rock, or foundation, on which He would build the foundation of His Church. Catholics recognize Peter as the first Pope, the leader of the Church instituted by Christ.

Jesus established His Church to unite all people through Him. Toward this objective, He left the Church in the hands of His appointed leader, Peter, and gave him the authority to carry on in His name. In anticipation of Peter's death, successors would be necessary to continue the leadership and teaching mission of the Church. Tracing historical accounts after Peter's death, we find a trail of leaders succeeding him. The trail leads all the way to the present Pope, Francis.

The Truth of God's Word never changes because it was given to us in perfection, but people are subject to imperfections. Jesus knew disputes, misinformation, and misinterpretation would crop up after He died. Help from Heaven would be needed to preserve and teach His word, not just for Peter, but for all time.

To make sure "the gates of Hades will not prevail against" the Church, it is only logical that a human leader, no matter what time in history, would need the supernatural, unifying assistance of God. As God granted infallible knowledge to Peter, the Holy Spirit still oversees the Church in the duty to keep Christ's teachings intact.

5. *I will give you the keys of the kingdom of heaven, and whatever you bind on earth will be bound in heaven, and whatever you loose on earth will be loosed in heaven.*

Jesus promised to give Peter the keys to the kingdom. The significance of this verse is tremendous, and I will not attempt to delve into every aspect. The simplistic presentation is: Keys represent authority. As Christ's appointed leader, Peter was authorized to put forth teachings, laws, and disciplines that "bind" the faithful appropriately to enhance the flock's spiritual health in keeping with Christ's teachings. With Christ's promise of the very special gift of the Spirit to guide the Church infallibly through Jesus' "main man," Jesus gave a very strong statement of trust by telling Peter that whenever the Church, through his leadership, decides to "bind" or "loose" something, the decision would stand in Heaven as well. Over the ages, this Spirit-inspired baton of authority has remained contained in the Church's teaching office (the bishops in union with the Pope) and is still in place today.

During Lent, for example, there are regulations pertaining to fasting and abstaining from meat that were put in place by the Church. Based on history and the many Scriptural references, fasting is good for our soul, so the Church sees fit to bind Catholics in unity to particular fasting regulations. Just as the Church is authorized to bind by law, it can also "loose" or change those same fasting requirements. In another instance of "binding," the Church has set various holy days of obligation in addition to the Lord's Day each Sunday. These days are in honor of special feasts of Christ, the Blessed Mother, or particular saints. They unite the faith community in celebration, thanksgiving, and commemoration. In communion with the Church, the faithful are bound to participate in Holy Mass on these special days.

Although Lenten fasting and holy days of obligation are indeed in harmony with Christ's teachings, they are not mandated from Heaven above, but are man-made regulations. Therefore, the Church can "loose" the obligations to the faithful if it seems appropriate. There are times, however, when a specific teaching has been proclaimed as a Truth born from the revelation of God. When the Church's teaching office hands down such a doctrine, all Catholics are bound to hold the teaching as true. Technically, the Church has the authority to "loose" a teaching if it is prudent to do so, but there would never be a need to "take back" a Truth. This is because Christ assigned to the Church the mission of teaching His Truth; and we trust His guarantee of supernatural assistance to forever preserve this Truth as it is being handed down. Using the God-given "papal infallibility clause" and the guidance of the Holy Spirit, the Church can do nothing but pronounce Truth when it comes to binding the whole Body of Christ in beliefs regarding faith and morals. The

Spirit's influence will forever intercede to prevent any distortion of the Truth from being officially proclaimed by His Church.

Any organization meant to grow needs leadership and authority, which allow it to operate in unity instead of division. Regulations are set in order to avoid chaos and malfunctions within daily operations. The same applies in family life. Parents lay down laws and assert leadership to run a smooth household in which children participate, learn, and thrive. The companies and organizations where we work and volunteer must have good managers to project and successfully accomplish goals. We look to our boss, our boss' boss, officers, and owners for authority and direction. We utilize pertinent, accurate information from those in charge, which allows us to go about our business efficiently and effectively. The Church must operate in a similar manner with appropriate directors to maintain an organization which is able to effectively shepherd such a large flock. Christ promoted leadership and authority within His Church. With the Pope, seated in the Chair of Peter — as the "chairman," if you will — the appointed cardinals and bishops and the ordained priests all function in organizational roles assigned to effectively build up Christ's Church with pertinent, accurate teachings. It should be a source of comfort knowing that we can go to "the top" with confidence when in need of illumination regarding our beliefs.

With Christ as the founder and head, the Church's mission is to proclaim and preserve Christ's teachings in the completeness He commands. The Church is motivated by obedience to His instructions to:

Make disciples of all nations, baptizing them in the name of the Father and of the Son and of the Holy Spirit, and teaching them to obey everything that I have commanded you. (MATTHEW 28:19-20)

The Catholic Church does not maintain a choke hold on all the gifts Christ proclaimed. This is precisely why the Church will forever pronounce to the world and share *everything* Christ embodied within her.

Christ prayed to the Father for unity of all people in belief of God and the Son He sent:

I ask not only on behalf of these, but also on behalf of those who will believe in me through their word, that they may all be one. As you, Father, are in me and I am in you, may they also be in us, so that the world may believe that you have sent me. (JOHN 17:20-21)

In this spirit of unity, a sense of duty calls the Church to continue to profess completely all that Jesus commanded and exemplified for the building up of God's people. In sync with Christ's prayer, the Church hopes that everyone, of all nations everywhere, will hear, investigate, and be drawn to embrace and take part in each and every gift Christ bestows upon humanity for the sake of uniting all to the fullness of Him.

EYE OPENER #4:   *Christ promised that the Holy Spirit would forever guide His Church in Truth.*

It is only through the promise and power of the Holy Spirit that the Church is able to carry out the tasks of preserving the fullness of Christ's teachings and communicating everything He set in motion. Jesus made His promises to the 12 Apostles at the Last Supper regarding the Holy Spirit:

And I will ask the Father, and he will give you another Advocate, to be with you forever. (JOHN 14:16)

I have said these things to you while I am still with you. But the Advocate, the Holy Spirit, whom the Father will send in my name, will teach you everything, and remind you of all that I have said to you. (JOHN 14:25-26)

I still have so many things to say to you, but you cannot bear them now. When the Spirit of truth comes, he will guide you into all the truth; for he will not speak on his own, but will speak whatever he hears, and he will declare to you the things that are to come. (JOHN 16:12-13)

After the Last Supper, Jesus explained to the Apostles that He would be going away. His death was imminent, but the Apostles did not understand the extent of all He was telling them. The promise of the Spirit of Truth was necessary to help the Apostles discern what Jesus taught them, remind them of all that He said, and to be with them always. Otherwise, without supernatural help, their lack of understanding as Christ departed would make it impossible for them to shepherd others in the completeness Jesus intended.

In addition to not fully comprehending the things Jesus already told them, He tells His Apostles there is much more to hear and understand, but it will have to wait for the future. He would soon send the Spirit to guide them in knowledge. The Spirit's job to forever guide in Truth and declare "things that are to come" applies to the Church today as surely as it did when Jesus originally made the promise. The Church is Christ's instrument to direct our way while journeying with God. It is precisely because of His promises that we can go with confidence to the Church for guidance.

Jesus also told His Apostles in preparation for His death and departure that:

Very truly, I tell you, whoever receives one whom I send receives me; and whoever receives me receives him who sent me. (JOHN 13:20)

Christ gave the Apostles authority to represent Him wherever they went to preach. The Pope, bishops, and priests have an apostolic lineage as shepherds sent out to feed His flock. When we receive the message of Christ through His representatives in the Church today, we are receiving and accepting Jesus, the Word of God. In following the desire to obey all that Christ passed down through His shepherds, we "receive" or accept the teachings of the Church, which continue to be set forth through the wisdom of the Spirit and the authority granted by Christ.

In some of his letters to fellow Christians, St. Paul referred to himself as "Paul, an apostle of Christ Jesus by the will of God." (2 Corinthians 1:1, Ephesians 1:1, Colossians 1:1) He made it clear that his mission in the early Church was assigned by God. Asserting his leadership, he wrote a letter to the believers in Thessalonica in which He stated:

So then, brothers and sisters, stand firm and hold fast to the traditions that you were taught by us, either by word of mouth or by our letter. (2 THESSALONIANS 2:15)

Paul's instructions apply to us. We are wise to hold fast to these same traditions and teachings handed down by mouth and letter to all generations through Christ's Church.

EYE-OPENER #5:   *The Spirit also guides individual members of the Body of Christ toward unity within the whole of the Body of Christ.*

We receive the Holy Spirit at Baptism. He dwells within us and guides us in our desires to follow Christ's teachings in our daily lives. The Spirit opens our eyes to Scripture so that we are able to apply God's ways to our decision making, our routines, our family life, our work life, our worship, and every other aspect of life.

As the years had me diving further into Christ's teachings in Scripture, I had to work through some of my concerns and questions. If the Holy Spirit was guiding me, why was it so difficult to make heads or tails out of Scripture when I began studying? Why did I twist some Scriptures to fit what I wanted to believe – as was the case when I equated one story to that of a positive pregnancy test? If the Holy Spirit speaks to each of us through the Bible, why do people of varying denominations have differing interpretations on some of what Jesus teaches through Scripture? Answers to these questions didn't hit me until after I began synchronizing my studies with the wisdom and guidance of the Church.

Playing connect-the-dots again, my mind was put at ease by contemplating and summarizing the "big picture" of how and why Christ founded His Church. He designed and founded His Church to be the caretaker of His Truth. He assigned this task permanently, through appointed leaders, to provide all generations with the completeness of every single one of His gifts and teachings. In order to assure that everything Jesus taught was carried forth as intended, God provided His Son's Church with the gift of papal infallibility; and Christ promised that the gates of Hell would not prevail against it. Boiling it down to one sentence is to say: the Holy Spirit would forever work through His Church to preserve and teach everything Jesus commanded *without altering or losing any of it.* Even though we may have the best of intentions and the desire to follow all that He taught, as individuals, we were not given this same infallible guarantee. Our guarantee kicks in when we count on the Church, which carries the guarantee through the Spirit to preserve His Truth, to assure us that our beliefs are, therefore, also infallible.

The Spirit works wonders within us in tandem with the Church. Papal infallibility is a unique gift of the Spirit given to the Church as a whole, not as individuals and not as individual communities. Individually, we have different gifts and talents, which are meant to be shared with others. We are each part of the Body of Christ making up the Church along with its leaders and shepherds. Strengthened and guided by the Spirit, we are meant to be fruitful working in unity as ligaments building up the whole of the body. This includes a unity in absorbing the Word of God. Within the Church's guiding presence, we have Christ's gifts of God-given authority, leadership, and wisdom to go to for pertinent, accurate information.

Christ died as He foretold. His teachings continued to be passed down through His leaders as He directed. Time moved along. Doubts and false teachings were cropping up in the faith communities as the Church grew and covered more ground. When false teachings were offered by Satan to Jesus in the desert, Jesus — filled with the Holy Spirit — successfully countered Satan with the Truth. Christ gave the Church the fullness of the Holy Spirit in order to successfully withstand the misinterpretations and false teachings that would continue to crop up, tempting us to chip away at the fullness of Christ's Truth.

St. Peter, Jesus' first chosen leader, addressed the Christian communities in a letter about the confusion over misinterpretations, doubts, and false prophets. (2 Peter) Peter reminded the faithful of Christ's great promises, which allow us to escape the corruption of the world, which allows us to always recognize Christ's Truth over the distortions of His Truth. He encouraged the disciples to count on Christ's Church leaders to provide the Truth as it is preserved by the supernatural power of the Spirit. Within this letter according to Peter, it is stated:

Therefore I intend to keep on reminding you of these things, though you know them already and are established in the truth that has come to you. I think it right, as long as I am in this body, to refresh your memory, since I know that my death will come soon, as indeed our Lord Jesus Christ has made clear to me. And I will make every effort so that after my departure you may be able at any time to recall these things. (2 PETER 1:12-15)

Peter is aware that the tendency to misinterpret God's Word will always be in the air. Even though Christians already knew Christ's teachings, some became confused and discouraged with doubt. Peter sees fit to continually remind them of all of the things the Savior preached. Peter asserts his Christ-given authority to continually prompt the faithful to live according to Jesus' full teachings. He also tells of plans to make sure the teachings are repeatedly stressed even after he's gone. In anticipation of his death, he vowed to put appropriate Church leadership in place to assure that the Truth lives on uncorrupted through the Spirit.

As it was before, it is now. Those earliest Christians went through the struggles of doubting and misinterpreting the Scriptures in spite of being given all that Christ handed down. Time has passed, but we still have these same battles today. Yes, the Spirit definitely works in each of us individually to guide our endeavors as we live the Gospel in our day-to-day lives. Yet, we are at times subject to confusion surrounding the intended and non-negotiable Truths handed down by Christ. This comes to light every day when we acknowledge the disagreements and varying interpretations of Christ's teachings that occur from one denomination to another; not just debates between Catholic and non-Catholic, but debates among Catholics and debates among varying Protestant denominations.

As one of Christ's Apostles, and His chosen leader, Peter's letter continues by telling the faithful that they should be respectful to the Church's teaching authority:

> *So we have the prophetic message more fully confirmed. You will do well to be attentive to this as to a lamp shining in a dark place, until the day dawns and the morning star rises in your hearts. First of all you must understand this, that no prophecy of Scripture is a matter of one's own interpretation, because no prophecy ever came by human will; but men and women moved by the Holy Spirit spoke from God.* (2 PETER 1:19-21)

We are not all experts in knowledge of Biblical history, culture, writing and speaking idiosyncrasies of the time. As individuals, and as faith communities, we are able to confidently trust the Church to confirm that we understand the full Truth of Scripture as God intended it to be for all time, for all people. With Christ's promise of the Spirit, which grants supernatural, papal infallibility to the Church, to preserve the Truth uncorrupted, we count on the Church to clear up confusion and doubts we may encounter as we go about our studies and weed through varying information. We as individuals do well to follow Peter's advice to be attentive to Christ's messages given through the Church, which shines on for all generations. When we find ourselves in need of answers, we are able to lean on our unity with Christ's trusted caregiver.

EYE-OPENER #6:   *The Church is not perfect in humanness, but Christ's promise will prevail through His divinity.*

Through the teaching office, which is the Pope in union with the bishops, the Church as a whole teaches the Truth and remains holy, but individual members are subject to error. That includes not only the lay people in the pews, but the Pope, bishops, priests, and other religious people who serve us. Even as Jesus went about establishing his Church through the chosen Apostles, He warned that not all of the disciples would always do what is right:

> *Jesus answered them, "Did I not choose you, the twelve? Yet one of you is a devil." He was speaking of Judas son of Simon Iscariot, for he, though one of the twelve, was going to betray him." (JOHN 6:70-71)*

Unfortunately, human weakness remains throughout the ages. Christ's warning was not isolated to Judas, but has played out in different stages of time. The threat of betrayal by some members of Jesus' Church will always exist because of human failings, not Christ's. Just as Judas' betrayal did not thwart God's plan of salvation through his Son, God will continue to preserve Christ's teachings by way of the Church His Son founded. Through Christ's promise of the Holy Spirit to infallibly guide the Church through papal leadership, the gates of Hell will not prevail against it.

As others began labeling me as a "church lady," I would receive remarks questioning my allegiance to a church historically scarred by scandal, including the sex abuse outrage that has come to the surface in our time. It must be understood that the infallibility of the Pope relates to divine assistance in carrying out duties as the teacher of all Christians regarding specific teachings with respect to faith and morals. It does not pertain to private morals, opinion, actions, theories, and choices. The Church is made up of people, just like every family, business, school, organization, city, and country in this world. God's family includes strong and weak individuals, most with good intentions. Individually, the pope and clergy are humans subject to flaws, unwise choices, and sin like the rest of us. As with all branches of society, misuses of authority have caused dissension among members. The Church, the Body of Christ, as a whole regrets such exploitations and works toward correcting and weeding out wrongdoing; but like a disease quarantined after the outbreak to control its spread, damage has been done.

My parish priest addressed his parishioners concerning a breaking story of a local priest arrested on child pornography charges. Father commented that at times like these he can feel embarrassment as a priest, but he has never once been embarrassed by his faith in Christ. When we are slapped in the face with wrongdoing by Church representatives, it hurts. Anger at a priest or parish member for less than stellar behavior or controversial statements is not a reason to abandon the entire foundation of one's faith. We must find consolation knowing that our perfect Christ is the center of our faith, that it is not the Church as a whole that has sinned, nor does the Church condone the behavior of the guilty individual(s). Let us remember the countless holy servants within the family that hold true to the image of Christ, but are not often mentioned for the sake of a scandal. Even when we hurt, we must reach beyond those displaying faults, and find peace in the fullness of all that Christ promised and commanded. Christ's Truth will break through any evil working to diminish solidarity with Him.

If you experience an occasion where a priest or religious person says something you don't think sounds quite right, find out what the official Church teaching or position is on the subject. The Catechism and the Vatican website are very helpful in this aspect. Our priests are under a lot of pressure and scrutiny to word everything just right for the massive number of ears listening. Remember that the Blessed Mother Mary asked the messenger Gabriel a question when she didn't understand his announcement that she would become the mother of God's Son. Our priests are God's messengers, too. Give them the benefit of the doubt and, if you have questions, ask for answers. Also, follow the sound advice to "pray to the Most High that He may direct your way in truth," and then do some homework to clear away any fog.

EYE-OPENER #7:   *Daily communication with God is essential to discovering and holding onto His Truth in its entirety.*

Prayer is a major factor in allowing the Most High to direct one's search in Truth. This communication makes the guidance and gifts of the Spirit more abundant as one comes to not only accept them, but to expect them. Before beginning any spiritual reading, research or meditation, I precede it by asking God to guide my endeavors.

Long ago, my initial efforts to heed advice to "meditate" went bust because the very word conjured up a picture of some complicated mode of special prayer tactics. Now, my understanding of meditation is letting God sit at the steering wheel of my mind where He can drive my thoughts on a tour that arrives at a deeper, Spirit-inspired view. Over the years, my prayer life has matured and blossomed, and I have confidence that it will continue to expand as God sees fit. A contributing factor to more effective reflection is when I take long walks in the park with my dog, Zeus. I so look forward to each walk because during that stretch of time, I am able to talk to God most intimately. We hike through the wooded trails where it is peaceful and not as busy with other walkers and distractions. What a gift for a person to discover what, where, and when is the best way for that soul to get lost in connecting with Him. I thank Him for drawing me into His arms so easily during my walks.

GOD EXPECTS ME TO BELIEVE

Blessed are those who have not seen and yet have come to believe. (JOHN 20:29)

EYE-OPENER #1: *We have a responsibility to seek information about Christ's teachings, handed down through His Church, that we question, don't agree with, or don't understand.*

There is much about the Father, Son, and Holy Spirit that remains a mystery with concepts defying human understanding. When I have difficulty grasping the way God works, I recall His message:

For my thoughts are not your thoughts, nor are your ways my ways, says the Lord. For as the heavens are higher than the earth, so are my ways higher than your ways and my thoughts than your thoughts. (ISAIAH 55:8-9)

There is also much about our faith that we base on history, reasoning, and revelation that promotes belief in the incredible mysteries of God. Before I gave a hoot about my religious roots, I had no curiosity as to why or how these teachings came about. Once my heart gained momentum in rekindling my relationship with my Creator, my brain had to dig into the long-ago connections and the reasoning behind what I held onto from childhood. Some of the convictions handed down to me did not make plain sense on their own standing; and it did not make sense that God, or the Church, would pull teachings out of thin air without some logical explanation. My persona is like a young child always asking "why." I needed to find the meat of these teachings. There was plenty to find.

EYE-OPENER #2:   *Jesus is truly present in the Eucharist – His body, blood, soul, and divinity.*

For all who eat and drink without discerning the body, eat and drink judgment against themselves. (1 CORINTHIANS 11:29)

My growing prayer life, understanding of my faith, and love for Jesus strengthened my relationship with Him in the Eucharist. Although my belief never faltered that He was physically present in the Eucharist, it was by faith alone that I held onto this "unbelievable" truth. My conviction was based only on the WHATs I had been taught as a child.

It was not until after my 25th high school reunion in 2001 that I set out to find the WHY surrounding the teaching of Jesus' true presence in the Eucharist. A childhood friend and I had been in touch concerning attending our reunion, and we met for lunch. TJ was raised Catholic, but as an adult she left Catholicism to join her husband's Lutheran church. During our luncheon we discussed some common beliefs and differences about our faith. My friend was adamant that the Catholic habit of worshipping "the host" made of bread was idol worship. My only response was that Jesus miraculously gave Himself to us in the form of bread as He explained at the Last Supper. I ended my comments by insisting that I adore Jesus, not any false god or idol. It was my inability to attach history or reasoning to my reply that was unsettling. Kudos to me for defending my faith, but how could I ever successfully explain why I believe such an incredible, but improvable, gift of faith. It became my mission to learn the WHY that goes along with the WHAT of the Eucharist.

My search began with the Catechism, which referred to Scripture. I was familiar with the initial Biblical reference I looked up because it is heard at every Mass. First, the priest calls upon the Holy Spirit to miraculously transform the simple, human offerings of bread and wine into the body and blood of our Lord. After this plea, the priest quotes Christ's instructions at the Last Supper:

> *The Lord Jesus on the night when he was betrayed took a loaf of bread, and when he had given thanks, he broke it and said, "This is my body that is for you. Do this in remembrance of me." In the same way he took the cup also, after supper, saying, "This cup is the new covenant in my blood. Do this, as often as you drink it, in remembrance of me." (1 CORINTHIANS 11:23-25)*

By faith alone, this should have been enough, but it was not enough for me at that point. There had to be more to the WHY. I looked further. "Further" was discovering what Jesus had to say in the Gospel of John, in particular Chapter 6. The following is a portion of the "Bread of Life" sermon given by Jesus to a crowd interested in what He had to say:

> *I am the living bread that came down from heaven. Whoever eats of this bread will live forever; and the bread that I will give for the life of the world is my flesh." The Jews then disputed among themselves, saying: "How can this man give us his flesh to eat?" So Jesus said to them, "Very truly, I tell you, unless you eat the flesh of the Son of man and drink his blood, you have no life in you. Those who eat my flesh and drink my blood have eternal life, and I will raise them up on the last day, for my flesh is true food and my blood is true drink. Those who eat my*

flesh and drink my blood abide in me, and I in them. Just as the living Father sent me, and I live because of the Father, so whoever eats me will live because of me. (JOHN 6:51-57)

Those listening to Jesus would have understood His words about the bread from Heaven in connection with the Old Testament story of Moses and his people fleeing Egypt. After that great escape, God's followers wandered the wilderness where they complained they had no food. Hearing their grumblings, God let bread-like manna fall from Heaven. His people ate it and maintained physical life, but Jesus was speaking of spiritual, eternal life.

Jesus' speech was in response to people asking Him to give them the life-giving bread He was touting so they could obtain eternal life. His answer was the WHAT of what they must do. Note that after the dispute arose, Jesus began His response with "very truly," thus telling the listener He was serious regarding what He was about to say. He was laying out the facts of the matter and giving a heads up on something profound. We'd best pay attention.

Nobody that day could appreciate Jesus' answer that He is the true bread from Heaven. They didn't comprehend what He was saying about eating His flesh. Not even His 12 Apostles could get a handle on Christ's remarks. Many disciples took offense and quit following Him after this sermon because the idea of eating flesh and drinking blood was ludicrous. To quote Scripture:

When many of his disciples heard it, they said, "This teaching is difficult; who can accept it?" (JOHN 6:60)

Jesus did not call the unbelievers back to apologize as if He were joking. Neither did He explain His words away as a parable. Jesus let them choose to walk away. Then He challenged His own Apostles asking if they too would leave:

Because of this many of his disciples turned back and no longer went about with him. So Jesus asked the twelve, "Do you also wish to go away?" (JOHN 6:66-67)

Peter answered Jesus:

Lord, to whom can we go? You have the words of eternal life. We have come to believe and know that you are the Holy One of God. (JOHN 6:68-69)

The Apostles stuck with Jesus not because they understood, but because their faith was strong enough to know He always spoke the truth. They trusted Him. It was not until later, at the Last Supper, when Christ instructed the Apostles on HOW they would do this incredible WHAT in the humble form of bread and wine.

Like the disciples who no longer followed Jesus back in His day, many today find His teaching on the Eucharist difficult, and they also reject it. I confess that being directed to eat and drink the body and blood of Christ sounds odd, but I never questioned the truth of this miracle. Although I was lukewarm in my younger days, I believed. Yet, I walked away. It wasn't because I found the teaching difficult, but more so because I didn't give it much thought. That is, at least not until my relationship with Him blossomed.

As I got to know Christ better, I wanted to make sense of God giving us His Son in the Eucharist by way of suffering and crucifixion. Jesus was born in the flesh to do the will of His Father, so the first thing I did was mull over what exactly was God's will. Christ summed it up quite nicely stating:

This is indeed the will of my Father, that all who see the Son and believe in him may have eternal life; and I will raise them up on the last day. (JOHN 6:40)

So, what did God's will have to do with the crucifixion of His Son? To answer this question, we must go back to the beginning of humanity. It was always God's plan that everyone enjoy eternal life with Him. However, when Adam and Eve disobeyed God, they forfeited the gift of eternal life and introduced death to the world. This eternal death sentence had to be countered to coincide with God's will that everyone may have eternal life. To fulfill His Father's objective, Christ took on the sins of all for the forgiveness of all. He was the only being worthy enough to make up for the consequences of wrongdoing once and for all. Along with the totality of sin, He physically took on the cost of sin, which was death. His earthly job ended when He died on the cross, conquering eternal death for humanity's sake. Jesus' last words before giving up His spirit were "It is finished" (John 19-30). Eternal life became obtainable once again. God's will was done.

Christ died to fulfill His Father's plan; but why the agony of it all? Why couldn't Christ have expired peacefully and still have the same impact on salvation? The final answer is that God could have done it any way He pleased. The goal of salvation could have been achieved had Jesus died a natural death, but that is not what happened. Time teaches that hatred breeds violence, and Jesus had enemies that wanted Him dead. Death by crucifixion resulted. We know that God would not will any evil act, so it was not His will that some would make the choice to brutally murder His innocent, beloved Son. He allowed the murder to be carried out based on the freedom of choice humans enjoy. Despite the cruelty and lack of human justice, God turned the tables on evil. He used Christ's death for the good of all, providing supreme justice in the end with the triumphant resurrection of His Son. The sinful murder of His Son did not thwart God's ultimate will. His promise of eternal life for all who see and believe remains intact. Also, Jesus' willingness to accept a vicious death, for crimes He did not commit, served to confirm His unlimited love for humanity in a way that is undeniable. He could have avoided the whole ugly experience by denying what He preached or by obliging taunts to "Come down from the cross now, so that we may see and believe" (Mark 15:32). He did neither. His suffering declared that all lives are worth dying for because they are sacred. Christ Himself said, "No one has greater love than this, to lay down one's life for one's friends" (John 15:13).

Along with the Bible and the Catechism, I read other books containing explanations of the many Scriptural references surrounding the Eucharist. Why God allowed such bizarre methods to bring about salvation became clearer as I read accounts of the Old Testament in connection with the New.

God's plan to present His Son as Savior had to play out in a way that made sense to people living in that era. In Jesus' day, Jewish society was steeped in rituals offering God sacrifices for the forgiveness of sins. The customs of His time included bloody animal sacrifices in keeping with the same Old Testament covenants as the forefathers. The offerings were accepted by God, but were repeated often because none were sufficient to make amends for all sin. These covenants also involved sealing the commitments between God and His people with the blood of the sacrificed animal. It follows that God sealed His covenant promise of salvation with sacrificial blood. That blood turned out to be the blood of His beloved Son.

Every fine, upstanding Jew living at the time of Christ knew the ancient stories of the flight from Egypt backward and forward. They knew that on the night before God freed His people from slavery, letting physical death pass over them, He gave His followers instructions. Details of God's directions for that first Passover are described in Chapter 12 of Exodus in the Old Testament and include:

- God's people must prepare a meal, which would include a sacrificed lamb without blemish.

- The lamb must be prepared and roasted whole without breaking any bones. The cooked lamb would be recognizable even in its changed state.

- God's people must eat the flesh of the lamb.

- The blood of the lamb must be sprinkled on the doorposts of each home where God's people dwelled, a sign of their attachment to the one, true God. This guaranteed physical life as the Angel of Death passed over their households.

God subsequently directed Moses that once a year, *for all generations*, His followers must commemorate as a *perpetual* institution how He saved them from death. Accordingly, each yearly Passover celebration must include sacrificing an unblemished lamb and the requirement to eat the lamb.

Fast forward to when John the Baptist identified Christ as the "Lamb of God":

Here is the Lamb of God who takes away the sin of the world!
(JOHN 1:29)

Aha! This is the connection between the Old and the New that clicked with me. I grew up hearing the priest call Jesus the "Lamb of God" at every Mass, but I never knew why. I thought it was because Christ was as gentle as a lamb. This title for our Lord finally made sense of the need, the gift, of eating the flesh and drinking the blood of the Lamb in the Eucharist. In accordance with His Father's covenant law with Moses — which directed His people to eat the flesh of the Passover lamb for all generations — Jesus, the Lamb of God, directed that it is His flesh that must be eaten because He is the new Passover Lamb. These specific events answered the WHY surrounding Jesus' acceptance of His death sentence as the "sacrificial Lamb," but also linked God's instructions to my own spiritual life through the Eucharist.

So then, we have covered the WHAT one must do to have eternal life through Jesus' explanation within His "Bread of Life" sermon, which taught that we must partake of His body and blood. Next, we looked at the WHY of Christ's sacrificial death in connection with salvation and eating of His body and blood. We will follow with the pieces leading us to HOW people for all generations will go about consuming this new Passover Lamb. Let's move on.

'Twas the night of the Last Supper. On this night before God saved His people from the slavery of sin, letting spiritual death pass over them, Jesus gave His followers instructions. He taught the Apostles HOW they would be able to consume His body and blood in the form of bread and wine. Jesus perfects and fulfills the Old Testament covenant with Moses, and will have the Apostles carry His New Covenant forward forever. The Apostles did not yet comprehend their role in the WHAT, the WHY, or the HOW.

Christ left that last meal and went off to Gethsemane to pray to the Father. He knew the events that would soon take place. It was here that He accepted the yoke of every horrible, unthinkable, humanly unforgivable deed that people are capable of committing, past, present, and into the future. He anguished over each single act of denial of His mercy and love that would take place — even after God would reveal Him as the Savior upon the cross. His physical torture had not officially begun, but Jesus' heart and spirit were in such agony as He prayed that His mental torment became physically apparent.

His sweat became blood. His bloody sweat sealed His agreement with the Father to proceed to the cross for the forgiveness of sin. He took the role of the Lamb being led to slaughter, and He sealed the deal with His own blood.

I was fascinated by the way God made sure that His Lamb would be recognizable as the promised Savior. Several simple details link Jesus to the instructions God gave Moses regarding the

Passover lambs. Among them, Jesus, the Lamb of God, is without sin. Therefore, He met the requirement as an unblemished, sacrificial lamb. Remember that God dictated to Moses that the bones of the lambs were not to be broken. Likewise, Christ's bones were not broken on the cross. The soldier aiming to break His legs to speed up death chose not to do so because Christ was already dead. Jesus is the Lamb that trumps all the previous lambs with His ability to take away sin once and for all. His blood was poured out just as the blood of the original Passover lambs was spilled to have death pass by.

It was after Christ's death and resurrection that the Holy Spirit opened the Apostles' eyes to the Old Testament Scriptures identifying Jesus as the new Passover Lamb. WHAT Jesus taught in the "Bread of Life" sermon about consuming His flesh and blood became lucid. The instructions given at the Last Supper were now crystal clear. It became obvious HOW they would be able to eat His flesh and drink the blood of the New Covenant within the humble, miraculous form of bread and wine. The Apostles became teachers of WHAT, HOW, and WHY we must eat the flesh and drink the blood of our Lord, Jesus Christ. The Catholic Church holds onto these teachings as the truth of the Bread of Life. The miracle of the Eucharist is the gift of the physical person of Christ given to all generations, including to you and to me. The Eucharist, under the appearance of bread and wine, is HOW we are able to physically accept Jesus as the literal Bread of Life and to eat the Lamb that must be consumed.

At Mass, the congregation expects to see the priest lift the consecrated Eucharist and say, "Behold the Lamb of God, behold Him who takes away the sins of the world." Every time we receive the Eucharistic Lamb, we participate in God's covenant, and obey God's perpetual Passover command to eat the Lamb. We have the opportunity to receive Jesus, the perfect, unblemished Lamb, at every Mass, in every Eucharist for all generations to come, forever. This reality takes my breath away.

Today, Christ the Lamb is recognizable to me in the changed state within the hosts of bread and wine. Not because the bread and wine look like Jesus, but because I welcome and recognize Christ within me. There are days when I am overwhelmed with awareness of my own changed state because of the body and blood of the Lamb of God. He is not only life-giving Bread, but He is life changing.

By the way, as God commanded Moses and His people to celebrate Passover with a sacrificial lamb once a year, Catholics are obliged to receive the Eucharistic Lamb at least once a year, preferably during the Easter season. This surprised me when I learned that the commitment was only once a year because we are required to celebrate Mass every Sunday and on special feast days. However, we are not to receive the Eucharist if we "examine ourselves" and are not reconciled to God. Prepared by the Sacrament of Reconciliation as needed, we are encouraged to receive the Eucharist at each Mass we attend, even daily if possible, for increased spiritual health.

About five years ago, I gave my friend Lois a rough draft of *God Expects Me*. Her occupation makes use of her sharpened professional writing and editing talents, and I asked that she use her expertise to seriously review my writings. She returned it to me with edits and comments that gave tremendous insight from a reader's point of view. Lois wrote a comment in the margin next to my statement: "The Apostles became teachers of WHAT, HOW, and WHY we must eat the flesh and drink the blood of our Lord, Jesus Christ." She asked, "Is there a slightly less barbaric way of putting this? – it makes me queasy!" The answer to Lois' question is "no." The words I used to describe the handing down of the Eucharist came from Christ's words. Her note made me imagine the scene at the Bread of Life sermon just after Christ told His listeners, "Eat my flesh and drink my blood." The followers who turned away probably felt queasy, too.

EYE-OPENER #3:   *The Holy Spirit is our power against unbelief.*

The same Spirit that guides the whole Body of Christ feeds the gift of faith – that ability to believe what we cannot see.

Without the gifts of the Spirit and of faith, there is so much about God that defies belief. Take for example, Christ's resurrection. For a man to come back from the dead after the third day is unbelievable even with today's technology. In Jesus' time, the hype over Christ rising from the dead would definitely breed doubt. There were plenty of witnesses to Jesus dying upon that cross. There were none that saw Him rise from death and walk out of the tomb. After Jesus died, the Apostles huddled together not knowing what to do next. They did not believe an overly excited Mary of Magdala when she told them He was alive again. Misgivings came from the very men that followed Jesus for three years of training. These were the Apostles expected to carry on Christ's mission, yet they were unsure. On the days when I am unsure, I look back at the Apostles' doubt, and I can relax. It happens to the best of people.

Jesus understood the fear and disbelief His human confidants were experiencing. He took care of it. He began appearing left and right, in flesh and bone, with hunger and thirst, and with all the tangible wounds of the cross. For 40 days He continued to appear to disciples to show them He was indeed alive. He reassured them, taught them more, and calmed their fears. Jesus didn't stop there. When the 40 days were up, He bodily rose into Heaven before the eyes of many. That should have removed any remaining qualms. Still, He knew all too well the temptations, doubts, falsehoods, and confusion that would emerge as the Apostles went about teaching God's Word. Christ also knew that they were not prepared to handle the job.

Because the Apostles were not prepared, Jesus instructed them to wait in Jerusalem until they received the "Advocate" that would empower them to carry on His work. The Holy Spirit descended upon them on the first Pentecost as they were gathered in a room together. Filled with the promised Spirit, their unbelief and fears disappeared, and their faith became rock solid. Now they were equipped to head out and build up Christ' Church with His teachings. Like the Apostles, none of us are ever ready to go out on our own without stumbling with fears and doubts of our own. We were made to take the Father, Son, and Holy Spirit wherever we may go. It is the Spirit that strengthens faith in times of misgiving. Faith is the gift that counteracts unbelief. Recall the words between Jesus and a father who brought his son to Him for healing:

The father: *But if you are able to do anything, have pity on us and help us.*

Jesus: *If you are able! — All things can be done for the one who believes.*

The father: *I believe; help my unbelief! (MARK 9:22-24)*

What a great, quick prayer in times of doubt, "I believe; help my unbelief!"

EYE-OPENER #4: *The gift of the Spirit is given freely, without bias, attempting to stir a response.*

Husband and I got together with Max and Lois after their return from a vacation in New Mexico. They share an interest in architecture and history, and New Mexico is bursting with both. The couple stopped at a little shrine in Santa Fe called El Santuario de Chimayo. The chapel was built in 1813 and from the beginning was associated with healings, pilgrimages, and a place to experience peace of mind and body.[2] Max and Lois were intrigued with the unassuming, archaic building. They entered the chapel to satisfy their architectural curiosity. Although their interest in the church was from an historical perspective, Lois knew I would be excited to hear about the visit. Aside from the fascinating design, Lois shared that she felt an exceptional peace within the walls of the chapel. She couldn't quite explain it. She thought it might be because of the simplicity of the church and the humble people in the area. Lois is not a believer, but my guess is that God introduced Himself to her. The Spirit had given her a hug with a sampling of the peace of God. What can I say? That's a believer's theory.

EYE-OPENER #5:   *Angels are real.*

> *For he will command His angels concerning you to guard you in all your ways. (PSALM 91:11)*

> *Take care that you do not despise one of these little ones; for, I tell you, in heaven their angels continually see the face of my Father in heaven. (MATTHEW 18:10)*

Some of the beliefs of the Christian faith are more simplistic than others. Take angels for instance. They seem to be a soothing matter of faith that many people whole heartedly embrace. When I was very young, I believed the notion that each person had their very own guardian angel. As I left childhood behind, I forgot about my angel and slowly let go of the things of God.

---

2 See website holychimayo.us for information on El Santuario de Chimayo

I didn't think about angels much at all for many years, but when I was 18, I did give mine a bit of consideration. I had gone to Ocean City, Maryland, with siblings and friends for an enjoyable, but exhausting, week-long vacation. On our last night at the ocean, we stayed up late enjoying a bonfire and lamenting the need to leave. Come morning, we packed up and prepared to make the journey home. I hopped into the driver's seat and off we went. We drove for hours. Everyone was sleeping except me. I was tired, so I rode with the window down. I changed the radio station. I dangled my arm into the air to feel the breeze. I changed the radio station. Now everyone was sleeping! The steering wheel jerked wildly in my limp hands to veer away from the cement barrier and back toward the road. My oldest brother slept in the back seat with his head leaned against the window. I woke up to the noise of his head as it bounced against the glass. My hands had not turned the wheel. My faith was in hibernation, but I knew it was my guardian angel that prevented a head-on collision into that barrier.

After participating in the prayer group, I regained an interest in reestablishing communication with my angel. By then I knew people who actually addressed their angels by name. Some of these folks arbitrarily assigned a name to their guardian. Others were positive God introduced them to their angel by name. My mother relayed that she simply asked God to reveal the name to her. It was during private prayer that Mom was graced with an answer. She was sitting on the couch reading Scripture. For a moment she closed her eyes to contemplate the passage. Instantly, a hand holding a rubber stamp flashed in her mind. The hand firmly brought the stamp down and then vanished. What remained was a name embossed in her mind's eye. The name was "Leia." This was not a common name she had floating around in her head. Mom understood this to be her angel's name.

After marveling at my mother's experience, I went to bed one evening with a plan to ask God to reveal my guardian's name. Worried I would subconsciously create a name while waiting for an answer, I asked Him not to tell me while I was wide awake. Otherwise, how would I determine if the name was coming from imagination or from above? *Please, God, tell me the name of my angel in the morning the first thing when I wake up. That's the best time because I'm too groggy to imagine anything except going back to sleep.* My prayer inferred that "the first thing when I wake up" would be when the alarm goes off to get me up for work. God took my words literally, and the first thing turned out to be 3:00 a.m. when I woke up to go to the bathroom. My body and brain were on automatic pilot to get to the bathroom and back to bed without truly waking up. As soon as my feet hit the floor to make the trek to the toilet, the name "Philip" crossed my mind. The alarm had not sounded yet, but God had introduced me to my angel. Angels don't have gender as we define it, but I fully expected that I'd have an angel with a feminine name. God used the unexpected so I would have no doubt. Trusting so profoundly that He told me my angel's name, I grumbled about it. *Lord, why did you pick Philip? I really don't care for the name at all. It was supposed to be a girl's name.* The name grew on me. I talk to Philip daily.

More recently, I was reflecting on that drive home from Ocean City so long ago. It struck me that my first awareness upon waking up was of my hands being limp. That's the detail that made me instantly certain I was not the one who turned the wheel. It astounds me that as a lukewarm, typical teenager, I unemotionally, without a second thought, knew my angel saved our lives that day. For the first time since I learned Philip's name, feelings about this event filled my heart. We are told it is never too late, so I thanked him profusely and showered him with gratitude for being my angel.

GOD EXPECTS ME TO GIVE HIM MY ANXIETIES

Therefore do not worry, saying, "What will we eat?" or "What will we drink?" or "What will we wear?" For it is the Gentiles who strive for all these things: and indeed your heavenly Father knows that you need all these things. But strive first for the kingdom of God and his righteousness, and all these things will be given to you as well. So do not worry about tomorrow, for tomorrow will bring worries of its own. Today's trouble is enough for today. (MATTHEW 6:31-34)

God tells us not to worry. When I first discovered this tidbit, I had difficulty with the concept. I didn't understand how I could possibly not be anxious. Doesn't anxiety come with your genes, the environment you exist in, and life in general? Yes, we all have cares and concerns, but we should not and cannot let them overtake us. Going to God has allowed me to keep anxieties in check and gives me the strength to move through them instead of falling under their weight.

EYE-OPENER #1: *God makes it possible to have peace in difficulties.*

In the early eighties, my brother Andy was diagnosed as a manic-depressive after demonstrating behavior that became increasingly bizarre as it led to his diagnosis. The stress on the family, especially on my parents and siblings still at home, was non-stop. Shortly after his diagnosis, I remember venting anger after a friend brought religion into the conversation. Being my "before-Christ self," I bluntly proclaimed there couldn't possibly be a God because any God that allowed such painful, awful things to happen in the world could not be who people say He is – all good, all loving, and all merciful. I didn't really believe my claim, but neither did I know how to deal with God on the rotten aspects of life.

Before Andy was diagnosed, he exhibited strong symptoms of mental imbalance, but our family didn't have a clue. He had various jobs after high school, none of which led to the money he aspired to earn. On a whim, Andy would sooner or later quit a job for one reason or another. At that time, we had no idea that certain stress levels were triggers for dormant symptoms of his illness to rush forth. So I labeled his antics "whims." He could feel it brewing like a storm. Andy didn't know there was a name for what he felt, but it didn't feel right. Running away from the stress was a method of keeping the worst from escalating. It was survival mode.

Even before Mom knew my older brother had this bipolar disorder, she had her own survival mode in place. She sought to keep the peace versus facing the issues head on. It was calmer to let her young adult son sleep all day and stay out all night in between jobs. On the other hand, Dad would endure until he could endure no longer. A mandate was given that Andy needed to leave home, find himself steady employment, and stand on his own two feet. This was the normal sequence of events for children to grow up and leave the nest. He flew the coop. He landed 1500 miles away in Texas working on oil rigs for a couple years before his first severe manic episode reached its peak. Shortly after checking himself into a hospital, being diagnosed, being put on temporary medications, and then being sent along his way, my brother flew home. My parents were formally introduced to manic-depressive illness when they picked up their son at the airport. At least he looked like their son.

It did not take long for us to get acquainted with the signs of bipolar disorder. Andy exhibited the manic side of the illness quite well by talking non-stop on dozens of different subjects within minutes, expressing brilliant ideas on becoming independently wealthy if only he had money to get started, being paranoid about spies, going days without sleeping, and setting a world record for pacing.

My parents took Andy to get help after he moved home. He received therapy and lithium from doctors and lots of care and love from Mom and Dad. Having no medical insurance, he volunteered for treatment through a program specializing in "medical discovery." Andy was given trial dosages of a drug and became a zombie. The program technicians somehow quit monitoring my brother, which left him on high dosages for an unprecedented amount of time. There came a point when he made the decision that he didn't want to live with the zombie-like side effects. He took himself out of the program and off the drug. Time marched on as it has a habit of doing. Andy marched on with some habits of his own. He self-medicated by drinking heavily and taking illicit drugs, which enabled him to live with himself. All family members were "enablers" because none of us knew how to deal with a mentally-ill addict. We did not face the reality of it. We danced around it and lived with it. Mom and Dad were smack in the middle of it.

Visits to see my parents always sent me home crying to Husband about the horrible situation, how lost my brother was, and how he was never going to change. Understandably, he had a difficult time living with an illness that society feared. Despite his disorder, Andy was intelligent enough to make better choices toward being the best he could be. Unfortunately, he gave up seeking a medical approach to battling his illness. Neither did he ask for divine intervention to see him through his struggles. Instead he sought to live on the seedier side of life. His choices allowed apprehension to flourish in the household, and its grasp extended to those surrounding him. Some were gripped by the disquiet more than others. Various names for the unrest might be sadness, depression, evil, or perhaps a living hell. The good news is that my mother countered the bad times the only way she knew. She turned to God. Signs of faith were everywhere. Mom had religious pictures and/or a crucifix in every room. She sprinkled holy water in Andy's bedroom when he wasn't looking. Mom invited God to assist in her helplessness because her son left an open invitation for Hell's angel to walk through her door. Belief in this supernatural God of light, in the Holy Spirit, in angels, and good spirits, brings with it belief in a supernatural Satan, darkness, and evil spirits. They are revealed in Scripture. They exist. Andy openly told me that he met the devil. Most times if someone declares to have met the devil, I would not take the statement literally. With my brother, I cannot totally doubt such an encounter.

Among attempts to change the situation, I would share my faith with Andy and suggest he pray for God's help. Sometimes I would confront him about being an alcoholic. He would admit it. There was a time when he wanted to go to Alcoholics Anonymous meetings, but he couldn't transport himself because he lost his license after a DUI. I offered to get him to the meetings. He accepted. Off we went. I offered to pay the fine to cover the DUI so he wouldn't be worried. He accepted. I paid the fine. My sincere efforts to help my brother heal his life were unsuccessful. After each attempt, I got knocked down with disappointment and uneasiness because Andy would phase into another sticky state of affairs.

Having grown to know the Lord better, I decided to try giving Him my anxieties. I gave Him Andy. The circumstances didn't change, but my despair lifted. My brother was in good hands. Finally I gave up trying to alter a situation that could only be corrected by Andy through the grace of God. He had to be willing to lift himself up. All the help in the world wouldn't help him stand on his feet if he wasn't willing to use his legs. I quit trying to fix life for my sibling, and told him the only thing I could give anymore was prayer. I experienced what it is like to have God take anxiety and replace it with peace. Nothing changed, but ultimately I came to a peace about my brother's illness by turning over my anxieties to God. I stopped crying.

I was not the only one praying for Andy. The situation was a call to prayer for the household. We sisters began gathering weekly at our parents' house to answer that call in unison.

In perseverance over the years, our prayers continue for Andy in his lifelong struggle with mental illness. We also pray that he will someday tend to his spiritual health as well.

EYE-OPENER #2:   *Asking God's help to conquer anxieties may be a daily activity.*

My experience with waning apprehension reminds me of the Scripture story where Joseph, Mary, and twelve-year-old Jesus were traveling home from Jerusalem after the Passover festival. Jesus was lost for three days as His parents anxiously searched for him. If I were Mary or Joseph, I know I would have been praying constantly over that journey, hoping not to fall apart with anxiety. After backtracking to Jerusalem, Mary and Joseph found their Son in the temple and their worry disappeared. (Luke 2:41-51)

Daily life has the potential to bring with it circumstances that can raise blood pressure and anxiety and leave us searching for Jesus. If we look, we will find Him. This finding must take place every day. Therein lies the peace.

One day in the not so distant past, I struggled to remember that I must call on God daily to have His peace because each day is a new day. We live in the present moment where the potential for change exists from one moment to the next.

The day began well, but peace was obliterated by about 7:00 p.m. that evening. Hannah called. She just hung up the phone after talking with Andy. He was at the convenience store where he worked, but at his wit's end with severe depression and thoughts of suicide. He had been fighting the depression for several weeks, but it continued to escalate. I called him. He wanted to leave work immediately. We talked through it. He decided he was able to finish his shift rather than endure the stress of calling his boss to beg him to return so Andy could depart. I assured him I would be there to pick him up after he closed at 11:30 p.m. I had plenty of time to pray, and I did. However, anxiety was rising up in my chest. My prayers were broken. I could feel anger brewing. My tone was agitated as I threw Scripture at God where it says we are supposed to be thankful in all circumstances. *OK, God. You are going to have to show me what I have to be thankful about in this circumstance because I sure can't see it. You were supposed to have taken care of this, but here we are again in a desperate state of anxiety and fear.*

I picked Andy up as scheduled, and we drove to the emergency room. We waited four hours while the staff took tests and evaluated my brother. The attendants assessed his condition and decided to admit him. A portion of my time at the hospital was spent in the waiting room to give Andy and his case worker privacy to talk. While sitting alone, my thoughts turned to my favorite flower, the rose. Roses have thorns. My heart softened. The tightness left my neck and shoulders. I thanked God for letting me be around to help my brother when he needed it most.

In the days ahead, peace came and went and came and went. Andy stayed in the hospital for about a week. I went to visit him a couple days prior to his release. He was still fretting about so many things. He worried that his boss would not take him back. He worried about paying the following month's rent and the utility bills if he had no job. He was upset that he may end up homeless one month into the future. For the finale, Andy admitted that he didn't know what he would do to himself if he went back to his apartment. I left the hospital extremely anxious over my sibling's future.

Different scenarios played over in my head. The possibility that I should take him into my home was a serious option. Allowing Andy to live with Husband and me would be fine for a week or two, but long-term it would create non-stop tension. Andy is high maintenance in his wants, needs, preferences, and compulsions with routine. He does not drive, he smokes heavily, and he would have no income or way to seek independence in the suburb where Husband and I live. Both of us work, which would make it difficult to taxi Andy around to find a job, let alone get him to work once he found one. I prayed and told God flat-out that I did not want to bring my brother into our home. I could only see the circumstances being very wearing on the mental, emotional, and marital health for Husband and myself, not to mention Andy's overall wellbeing. Furthermore, I informed God that if Andy moved in, I didn't see him moving out. Neither did I want him out on the streets somewhere. What would Jesus do? I prayed for His help with this major decision.

It was the evening prior to Andy's release. My peace was gone. I saw no other way to ease my mind than to invite my sibling to live with us. His life was at stake. During the hour-long ride to the hospital, I prayed some more. *Please, Lord, is this the right decision knowing the unrest that will take hold?* I arrived at the hospital. The way to Andy's room was paved with security measures and locked doors. One of the counselors on duty buzzed me through to yet another set of iron doors. As she led me to Andy's quarters, I impulsively engaged the woman by asking why my brother was being released when his state seems unstable and suicidal. She was upfront in explaining that during Andy's stay, he was invited every day to participate in group activities and therapy to help his mood. He declined. Advice was offered that he should call his boss to discuss the circumstances. He was given toll-free numbers to contact the utility companies about his situation. He made no calls. Medically speaking, clinically depressed persons are not able to concentrate long enough to read for five minutes. Andy stayed in his room and read three books over several days. It was professional opinion that he appeared to be manipulating the situation to make things easier on him. In her personal opinion, he was hoping I was the angel that would drop in to scoop him up, take him home, and allow him to lay back, read, relax, and leave responsibility behind.

Thanks, God. My decision was made. My peace returned. I walked back to Andy's hospital room with confidence. As we talked, I informed him that I could not take him home to live with me. We had serious conversation about his life. I reminded him of all he had established in the town where he lived. He was independent and well known because of his job. Without a car, he walked the couple miles to work and was in good shape because of it. He also had the advantage of a reliable bus line that was convenient when walking was not. The doctors he routinely saw for checkups and medicines were along that route. Moving in with me would remove all that he had access to and had accomplished because of it. I made it clear that it would not be healthy for him, my husband, or me to have him become totally dependent on us. Then I advised him to quit answering his own questions by telling himself that everything he needed to succeed was a "no." Instead, get reliable answers by calling his boss, the utility companies, the landlord, and the hospital social worker to ask if they would work with him. Before I said goodbye for the night, I told Andy that I would research local shelters to find some on his bus route that might offer classes or employment coaching. If it comes down to finding a new home in a shelter, I would drive him to each one so he could talk to the managers and decide on the best match for him. He had a lot to think about before checking out of the hospital.

The next day, I called my brother to see what time he would be discharged, and offered to give him a ride. There was no need. He had made an appointment to see his psychologist and would take the bus to the doctor's office and then home. Andy also talked to his boss, who told him to focus on getting better and return to work when he was ready. He called the utility companies, his landlord, and the social worker. Everything was under control and plans in place. Andy was on his way once again to independence and simple living.

God walked our family, slowly I might add, through Andy's episode of severe depression. With assistance from family and friends to get to the grocery store, the laundry mat, or the bank, he managed. It took over a year of trial and error with different medications, but eventually a combination was found that stabilized his brain chemistry.

Andy battles the odds of success and provides a living for himself and strives to remain independent. During one telephone conversation, he was down about the prospect of being a cashier at the same convenience store for another 20 years. I countered his viewpoint with a look at the facts of the matter. Most people don't struggle with bipolar illness while trying to make it in a society that has no patience for such things. He holds a steady job, maintains his independence, and lives in a small apartment that suits his needs and tight budget. God is pleased when we live simply. Andy does a very good job of that. Most of all, he seems at peace with life for the first time in a very long time.

Looking back at the change in my anxiety level between the time of Hannah's phone call until the time Andy left the hospital, I thought about my exchanges with God. I went to Him with anxiety, with anger, in prayerfulness, then strength, and in peace and calm. My conversations with God were like those with a close friend that I can call on for everything and be honest and open about my concerns. I found Jesus during those varying moods of prayer and the end result was my Friend calmed me down and left me to trust in His care.

EYE-OPENER #3:   *Sometimes anxieties are of our own making.*

Jesus wants us to go to Him with our worries instead of carrying the burdens alone. Just as surely, He also doesn't want us making mountains out of mole hills.

About a year ago, I had a conversation with a priest at a dinner benefiting students at his parish's school. One of Father John's favorite Scriptures is from the Gospel of Luke in which Jesus is visiting the home of friends, Martha and Mary:

> *Now as they went on their way, he entered a certain village, where a woman named Martha welcomed him into her home. She had a sister named Mary, who sat at the Lord's feet and listened to what he was saying. But Martha was distracted by her many tasks; so she came to him and asked, "Lord, do you not care that my sister has left me to do all the work by myself? Tell her then to help me." But the Lord answered her, "Martha, Martha, you are worried and distracted by many things; there is need of only one thing. Mary has chosen the better part, which will not be taken away from her." (LUKE 10:38-42)*

Our dinner conversation touched on Jesus' response to Martha's anxiety about serving Jesus without any help from her sister. Father John pointed out that the Lord did not get drawn into Martha's drama. Jesus did not take on her anxiety because it was an unnecessary distraction, and He lovingly taught her so. Martha was focused on serving our Lord, which is a very noble task we are all called to do. However, her focus became a distraction to the more important fact that she was in the loving presence of our Lord. It would have been more beneficial for Martha to enjoy the moment of Christ's company and put the serving in perspective. The insight Father shared touched me because I used to have an unhealthy obsession with cleaning, scrubbing, and cooking whenever company was coming. I made myself so anxious about having everything perfect that when the guests arrived, I was still tense about being the perfect hostess. I had trouble sitting, relaxing, and enjoying friends and family. Instead, I'd be up and down worrying about every little detail, crumb on the floor, or dirty dish. My own sisters have taught me to not be so "distracted" as Martha was about serving. I am now better able to put the focus where it belongs — on Christ and on people — instead of secondary, non-essential things that come into play.

Minimizing distractions to enjoy time with the Lord will help keep our mole hills from becoming mountains. Learning to prioritize and moderate life's activities rather than give them extreme attention and obsession will allow more time to give God the prime role in our lives, which He deserves and we need. Like Martha, who almost missed the reality of the precious gift of Jesus sitting in her living room, we only need look around us in the present moment to find Jesus. Sometimes, like Martha, we need to be taught to recognize Him in our midst and to prayerfully sit at His feet to keep our mole hills in check.

It took me a long time to realize my days were ruled by plans of the future. My thought process tended to always map out tomorrows and dwell on the worries of living life. Whether the event or problem was big or small, a day away or a year away, I did not realize how my focus over what's next prevented me from breathing in the refreshing beauty of the here and now. Recognizing what I was doing, I began to pray for help in seeing the simple joys that God provides on a daily basis. It was very freeing when I began to find myself soaking in the joy of present moments. Moments that made me automatically smile inside and out. Moments like: enjoying the sun pouring through the clouds just after a morning rain, spotting a mother doe and her little ones off on a hillside, sharing conversation with my nephew, Michael, while teaching him how to make my infamous blueberry pancakes, or holding hands with my husband as we walk to the car. One momentous occasion happened on a morning walk as I looked up at the sky and exclaimed, "There's not a cloud in the sky." Being 50 years old at the time, to hear myself properly use that old, worn out saying as a reality of the beauty God provides each day was a source of enlightenment and joy.

EYE-OPENER #4:   *When bad things happen, God will lead us from the hurt into the good.*

One particular Scripture provides consolation when it comes to dealing with the overwhelming struggles life dishes out:

I am the vine, you are the branches. Those who abide in me and I in them bear much fruit, because apart from me you can do nothing. (JOHN 15:5)

None of us are exempt from periods of pain and anguish while we go about business on Earth. Some people experience indescribable hurt or sorrow that leaves the emotions so numb inside that they "can do nothing" for a period. The damage of life's storms is not cleaned up overnight. Healing is a process. It takes time. When a child of God's is deeply hurt, and feeling as if they can do nothing, He will carry that person through, allow healing, and provide the ability to "bear much fruit" that will squash the residue suffering leaves behind. Embracing our loving Father means we can run to Him for help. In response, He empowers us and brings forth talents we didn't know we possessed. We become models of focus, fortitude, energy and determination and accomplish things we never thought possible. We carry on to contend with what otherwise might have crippled. There are many reports of this phenomenon. Parents who have lost a child to cancer go on to raise funds to help families going through the same fight. Victims of violence will grow to counsel others escaping abuse. Al-Anon and Alcoholics Anonymous are both based on people who convert their weaknesses into a gift by helping others with similar burdens. Individuals tend to offer empathy and assistance to other people going through a crisis similar to what they have experienced and survived.

My Goddaughter, Molly, turned into a young adult before I knew it. Like me, she asks questions about life. Once in a blue moon, we are able to walk Zeus together at a nearby park. It's a peaceful, relaxed atmosphere that allows us to talk uninterrupted until we reach the end of the trail and head for home. During one of our chats, we got on the subject of God bringing forth good even from bad circumstances. Molly asked me if that was the same thing as "everything happens for a reason." I had to stop to think for a moment. At the same time, I silently invited God to join the conversation. Many people refer to this saying when they console someone going through a rough time. My first inclination was to say "yes," but that didn't quite ring true for me. It implies that if a horrible crime takes place, there must be a good reason that it happened, but it isn't apparent yet; or if a baby is killed in a car accident because of a drunk driver, there must be good in that; or if a person cheats on a spouse, that spouse should realize there must be a better plan. My answer to Molly's question was "no," and I offered her an explanation. When "the bad" occurs, "the good" does not exist in the same time slot. "The good" takes time to be drawn out of the experience, often after healing takes place. In my opinion, "everything happens for a reason" is too generic. It allows us to push God out of the picture. That expression is not at all the same as God can bring good out of bad. I confess that as a young adult, it did not make sense that good could come from evil. I thought that a true God would prevent evil from happening in the first place. As I matured in my knowledge of our Creator, I realized that evil is not born of God, but from the choices made by humans. He does not give permission for people to sin against others, themselves, or Him in any fashion. Nor does He want or will evil actions to take place so that He can pull good out of them. No. Evil does not happen for any good reason at all. Yet, when a child of God endures "the bad," the Father will provide graces that allow healing and strength, and he or she will go on to "bear good fruit" made possible by the grace and mercy of God.

As I was trying to understand more about the ways of God, another question I asked myself was, *Why does He let natural disasters such as disease, floods, tornadoes, and more happen that cause pain, suffering, and anxiety for His people?* To answer this, I had to go back again to Adam and Eve. None of this suffering was in God's original plan for His people or any of His creation. He willed that we share in His eternal bliss from the beginning, which allowed humanity, the animals, the seas, the skies, the land to exist in peace and harmony side by side. It was the disobedience of Adam and Eve that allowed disharmony between humanity and nature to take seed and thrive.

Nature is not evil in itself, but it certainly can wreak havoc in our lives. We continue to suffer the snowballing consequences of that first sin by our ancient ancestors, and we are subject to the existing laws of nature and physics.

Although actions and events happen that are not willed by God, they are allowed to happen because the perfect, blissful harmony offered by God was freely rejected. If we run to Him in our own disharmony, He will lead us to conquer our anxieties and hurts by taking us to the good. There will be peace.

EYE-OPENER #5:   *Following the prescription to love God and others leads to the internal peace we seek.*

My level of angst can be charted according to my relationship with God at a particular point in time. The fuller I was with self-motivation, the less room there was for the commandments of loving God and my neighbor. Coinciding with a heart full of self was a chest full of anxiety. As time opened me up to portion more and more room for God, family, and others, my level of unrest went way down. When I shared these thoughts with Husband, he responded with wisdom. His vision of the perfect heart would have only one portion, which would be one filled to the brim with love of God. When one is totally full of God's love, "others" and "self" are contained within. That person would already be moved to love and serve and have the proper form of self-love. As anxiety tries to overtake a heart given over to God, He absorbs it.

Putting into practice this total giving of one's heart to God in every situation is not automatic. To get to that point of constant trust and love requires prayer and perseverance. God wants to take each and every one of us there. We must be willing to commit to the going.

GOD EXPECTS ME TO FORGIVE THOSE WHOM I CAN'T

For if you forgive others their trespasses, your heavenly Father will also forgive you; but if you do not forgive others, neither will your Father forgive your trespasses. (MATTHEW 6:14-15)

EYE-OPENER #1:   *Forgiving others is not optional.*

Most Christians commit, whether wittingly or unwittingly, to the above Scripture in Matthew every time the Lord's Prayer (The Our Father) is said. Within this appeal we tell God:

And forgive us our debts, as we also have forgiven our debtors. (MATTHEW 6:12)

Not only are we asking God to forgive us, but we are agreeing that He can forgive us, or not, according to how we forgive those who have hurt us.

There was a period of time when I conducted a weekly Bible study at a prison for teenage boys. (I will share more about this ministry in a later chapter.) I recall the comments of a particular attendee during one of these sessions. This young teen was sentenced to the correctional institution for crimes in connection with gang activities, which most likely included drugs and violence. During one lesson, we discussed Christ's command to love thy enemy. I remember so vividly how this gang member laughed sarcastically, but every bit as seriously, at how impossible it is to forgive an enemy in real life. He said that I didn't understand how he always had to "watch his back" or he'd be killed. There was no way he could ever love those who hate him. I agreed that I didn't quite understand, but Christ did. As He was nailed to a cross and dying, He spoke these words regarding His enemies, "Father, forgive them; for they do not know what they are doing" (Luke 23:34). This He prayed after being beaten, mocked, tortured, and left to die. For all who suffer violence against them, Christ serves as proof positive that it is possible to pardon those who have violated the sanctity of another's life. Through God it becomes possible.

A young prisoner named Alex regularly attended my first Bible study series. His face is seared into my memory from the day he shared with me experiences about his life. He mentioned he drank a warm glass of milk every night. I asked him if his ritual helped him sleep. Alex casually told me that it didn't really help much. He went on to relay a story that caught me off guard because his sleepless-ness reflected life for him and his younger sister. His mother was an alcoholic who became abusive when intoxicated. She had divorced, remarried, and the family moved into the stepfather's house. On the days when his mother was terribly drunk and still awake, Alex would round up his sister and get her out of the house for her protection. On nights when the stepfather was terribly drunk, he would enter Alex's room and rape him. When Alex told me this, he had to spell "r a p e" because he could not say the word. He couldn't sleep because of nightmares. I'm certain Alex never pictures himself forgiving his mother and stepfather. It is only through the grace of God that it would become possible.

Daily news reports include horrific, unthinkable crimes committed against adults and children alike. Hurts that perhaps have never been spoken, never healed, never forgiven. I believe a person can reach a point where it is not humanly feasible to forgive. It may not be humanly so, but it is possible. Recall that it is required by God to forgive those who trespass against us. English poet, Alexander Pope wrote, "To err is human; to forgive, divine."[3] Seeking divine intervention may be the only way to obtain the capacity to forgive. Anyone in need of the ability to divinely forgive another should solicit God to grace them with this gift. Persevere in this request. Be confident that He will carry you through any struggle to forgive. Trust Him to lead you to success in the matter because He expects it of you.

Forgiving another does not make it necessary to embrace the offender as one would embrace a best friend. It does mean loving the offender by letting go of the anger. Forgiving can be at a distance. For example, if a person wants to forgive an estranged spouse for physical abuse, it is not required to have face-to-face contact with the violent person. It is not necessary to enter into harmful situations in order to forgive.

Forgiving is not for God's sake, but for human sake. God knows that forgiveness must take place for the festering to stop. True forgiveness has taken place when peace replaces the unrest within one's soul. As seen by Christ's example as He absolved His tormenters from the cross, mercy can be shown by praying for offenders. Let us turn to Him for the ability to pray for and to forgive our own tormenters.

Nothing is impossible with God.

EYE-OPENER #2:   *It is necessary to forgive yourself.*

It has been a long time since I was drawn back to receiving the sacrament of Reconciliation as an adult. That experience was not how I remembered receiving the sacrament as a child. Making that "first confession" as an adult, I stood in line with a hundred

---

3 Alexander Pope (1688-1744), *An Essay on Criticism,*1711

others. The line was not to enter the traditional, private confessional. Rather, I waited to reach the priest standing openly in front of the altar. To loosely define this concept is to say that I didn't have to "do the time," but only had to quickly whisper to the priest one burdensome sin. It took but a second. I moved along, and the next person in line took the next second, and so on. As an immature convert searching to know Him, that impersonal absolution was sufficient for the moment. However, it apparently had limitations when stacked against the wisdom of confessing personally and privately to a priest. I wouldn't realize this until much later.

Time is a teacher. It took many years, even after my love for God had deepened and matured, for me to conceptualize that my days had become filled with deep sorrow. I became intensely aware of how much I had dishonored the Lord in my pre-Christ life. Like Adam and Eve when they felt shame after disobeying Him, I became conscious that I was unclothed before Him every time I approached the altar. I was ashamed. Harboring increasing remorse for my offenses created an invisible wall that I could not climb. That wall prevented me from moving forward in a relationship with my heavenly Father.

I was going to confession quite regularly during these years. I understood the teaching of God's mercy and the forgiveness of sins, but something was wrong. It slowly crept up on me. It grew more intense. Each day I would end up crying silently to God about how I couldn't stand myself for living so much of life without Him. It dawned on me that everything I learned as a child about what God expects was meant for my own happiness and wellbeing. It was all meant to allow me to build a strong, loving relationship with our Father and others, which would take me to being the best I could become. I ignored it all for so long, and I was now looking at the trail of disappointment I left Him. The extreme self-loathing was pulling me back from Him. I found myself losing grip on the invisible rope God throws us, and I was sliding backwards on that wall between me and God. There was no peace. It was inevitable that He would open my eyes to how crippled with regret I had become. My prayers began to scream out for help to overcome this daily fall.

It was while attending a yearly retreat with women from my parish that the bubble burst. During this particular retreat, I spent much silent time in the chapel. My prayers included asking for the grace to move forward spiritually. Without question, in my ignorance and sincerity in that general confession years ago, God absolved my sins and accepted my apology, but I was missing the peace that should accompany that knowledge. I found what was missing when I finally felt the fruits of a truly purifying, private, individual confession to a priest. I did not need hours in the confessional to account for the burden within me. Within a short dialogue, I was able to sum up my sorrow and feel the cleansing. The human need to "let it all out" was met. It was after that one-on-one conversation with Christ's priest that I was able to embrace God's unconditional love and mercy, wrap myself in it, and forgive myself.

Parents love unconditionally even when children provide worry or disappoint over their choices and actions. Our Father above never quits loving us if we go off on our own without Him. Like our earthly parents, He celebrates when we finally "get Him" and return to let Him know it. It's a new day.

EYE-OPENER #3:   *God's mercy is not a one-time occurrence. It is constant.*

As years have gone by and my spiritual maturity increased, my experience as a sinner only magnifies my appreciation and gratitude for the gift of mercy God bestows upon us. I am also very aware that we all slip and fall even amidst the excitement of a loving relationship with our Creator. History repeats itself, and at times I still need a reminder of the tremendous gift of grace we have in the sacrament of Reconciliation.

After rediscovering the sacrament of mercy, I had been drawn to confess at least once a month. The rejuvenation afterwards was always a source of closeness to Christ. Although the Church encourages us to receive this sacrament often, it is not mandatory unless one has committed a grave sin. For whatever reason, my inclination to confess waned for a period, and I was only stepping into the confessional once a year. I would often put it in my mind to go this day or that day, but once the time slot came about, I didn't make good on my promise. I wasn't in the mood. I was not in the state of serious sin, but I had gone into denial regarding the little sins that add up over 12 months.

As a child, I remember learning that sin turns us away from God. This includes not only things I did that I shouldn't have done, but the things I should have done, but didn't. Even modest sins cut Him off a bit at a time making one prone to future offenses. In my adolescence, I knew this simple definition of sin, but it never hit home in my heart. Now, all grown up, I became sensitive to this observation. I had lost some of the excitement of talking to God each day, or more accurately, I was having trouble praying. I'd start to talk to Him, but abruptly quit because the vibes weren't right. My day was more blah, I was irritable, the joy of simple moments passed me by, and I would accuse God of not being my God since I was not "feeling it" most days. In staying away from Reconciliation, I kept slipping off that invisible wall leading to Him. Instead of grasping the invisible rope He throws to help me climb, I held on tight to an attitude stirred by sin. Subconsciously, I believe I was aware of avoiding His help to lift me up. I wasn't in the mood to take His hand. As hard as it is to admit, sometimes I wanted Him to quit bothering me. I put myself in danger of severing that very personal, daily friendship piece by piece. It was not God who let me slide. It was my own doing. God always calls us into His embrace ready to lift us up with grace, mercy, and love. Sometimes we are blind to His help or downright stubborn about accepting it. As the saying goes, "If God seems far away, who moved?"

Two years ago, I participated in my first "The Light is on For You" service, which was a three hour celebration of the sacrament of Reconciliation. It took place in all churches of the diocese and invited all Catholics, whether lukewarm, cold, or hot, to take part. Again, I wasn't in the frame of mind to go, but I was determined to make my annual visit. Our bishop presided that evening along with the pastor. The lines that formed outside of each cleric's confessional room were substantial. My wait was two and a half hours, but it was well worth sticking it out. During the delay I had sufficient time to pray and to ask the Holy Spirit for guidance in making my confession. I also took the opportunity to read a pamphlet available with hints on how to make a good, sincere confession through examination of conscience. This well written leaflet slapped me in the face with food for thought that I hadn't given consideration. Two plus hours put me in a position to truly prepare to repent. The previous few years in which I only dutifully confessed, I did not give myself time for pause and readiness before confessing to Christ's representative. I was bypassing a necessary step in asking forgiveness. No wonder I wasn't looking forward to the experience. I had been setting myself up to take for granted God's forgiving nature. I was like a college student hitting the books five minutes before a final. This time it was different because I gave of myself 100 percent as a willing participant in this exchange. I came out of the confessional renewed. I had been cleaned up by the grace filled shower of God's love and mercy.

God have mercy. I slipped again. The news broadcast came across the air informing viewers of the bombing in Boston at the 2013 annual marathon. One suspect was shot and killed during a spray of gun fire while the second escaped. A photo of the escapee glared at me from the left side of the TV screen. My thoughts were that I was glad the first man was killed, and I hoped the second man was scared to death about the manhunt taking place to find him. It was in me to want him dead. My next thoughts, *Forgive me, Lord. Help me to forgive him; help the world to forgive.* Then I asked Him to help me pray for the killer's soul. I thanked God that I had it in me to seek His help to forgive. Even as I did so, it was not an easy prayer. I also prayed that my heart would sincerely be able to pray for even the most hardened criminal because He wants every person to accept His mercy and join Him eternally.

The name of that rope God has hanging over the invisible wall to eternal life is Jesus Christ. God's Divine Mercy has the same name. The wall does not really exist, but is an obstacle of our own making through sin and apathy. The message of His unfathomable mercy has always existed, but we either don't understand it, ignore it, or don't feel worthy of it. He does not want to lose one of us. For our sakes He extends so much grace, love, and mercy to make it near impossible not to join Him eternally when our time comes. The severe problem is that we don't take Him up on it all. He's expecting each one of us to knock on Heaven's door, but we must seek His help to break down the wall of obstacles.

GOD EXPECTS ME TO BE CLAY

Yet, O Lord, you are our Father; we are the clay, and you are our potter; we are all the work of your hand. (ISAIAH 64:8)

My heart, mind, and spirit had been tainted from years of leaving God out of my life. As my spiritual health improved, I gave Him permission to mold me to be what I was created to be all along. Constantly I turned myself over to Him as clay and asked Him to be my potter. I wanted to be a reflection of Christ, but I wasn't yet aware of how much restoration was needed. He slowly obliged me by allowing conversion to take place in his all-knowing, timely fashion. Perhaps my transformation is more accurately defined as peeling away layers of bad habits, bad attitudes, and bad information accumulated while living life. I was being debugged!

EYE-OPENER #1: *God takes our hands to walk us through transformation and growth.*

Making the metamorphosis into an adult Christian is not always easy. It can be scary to change. We may not know how to go about it or know exactly what needs to be altered. It is not essential to know ahead of time. All we have to do is give God permission, and He will orchestrate the necessary grace along with the proper self-awareness. He will allow each person to transform at a pace right for that individual.

Every Christmas season, Husband and I watch the 1970 animated TV special "Santa Claus is Coming to Town" (Rankin/Bass). One of my favorite parts of the story is when the Winter Warlock and Kris Kringle meet face to face. At first, they are at odds because the Warlock has a mean, cold heart. Kris shocked Mr. Warlock by giving him a gift, which no one had ever done before. Kris' gesture was enough to warm the creature's heart and the icy version melted away.

Mr. Warlock allowed his heart to open up to change. He even wanted to soften his name and asked Kris to call him "Winter" instead of Mr. Warlock. Through Kris' example of kindness, Winter also receives self-awareness and admits that he has been mean to those who dare tread near him. As they sing "Put One Foot in Front of the Other,"[4] he and Kris delve into Winter's strong desire to change. It comes out in this musical conversation that Winter was afraid that his wish to have a better outlook was only temporary. Because his heart was so habitually hardened, Winter worried it would be too difficult to transform. At the same time, he regretted his past wrongdoing and truly wanted to be reborn. Kris assured the beast that it's easy to change and anyone can do it. Kris taught his new friend to start small, take one step at a time. Then there is no need to be overwhelmed. Winter happily comes to the realization that it is in him to choose to do good instead of evil. All he had to do was be determined to get started.

And so it is with each of us no matter how mean and hardened we have been in the past. All we have to do is make a simple choice to change what we don't like within the mirror of our souls. Once we respond to God with even a tiny step toward Him, giving permission to awaken us, we will be reborn, recreated according to God's original blueprint before all the worldly distractions. Take the first step first. Ask God to orchestrate. Let Him. He will. Trust Him.

---

4 Maury Laws, Jules Bass, *Santa Claus is Coming to Town*, (Ontario: Rankin/Bass Productions, Inc., 1970)

My own first steps in walking with God were slow, but they served to move me in the right direction. Toward the late nineties, I began asking God to bring to the surface what I couldn't see on my own. In hindsight, I'm convinced He answered my prayers with the gift of self-awareness. Like the Winter Warlock, self-awareness picked up the pace for my own transformation. In my experience, the Lord seemed to bring up one issue at a time for me to ponder. Then, aware of the need and desire to change, I would call on my Potter to assist in molding another piece of me closer to the image of Christ.

One of the modifications I desired within myself was to love God better. I wanted to worship Him the way God should be revered, but I wasn't quite sure what that entailed. Attending Mass was one way of worshipping in unison with the community, but it felt like I had an overly routine attitude as I sat among His people. I strongly wanted to treat Him more like "THE God" and be in total awe of this supernatural being. It irked me that I treated Him so ordinarily. So, I prayed to be in awe of this gift of Jesus, my God, in the Eucharist.

At a Sunday Mass soon after making this request, I received the Eucharist and knelt with my head in my hands to pray. A specific thought shot through my mind like lightning, *Jesus, I **am** touching your cloak. Heal me!*[5] No sooner was the prayer thought when my eyes became teary. It was God again. This was between Him and me. It was extraordinary because it was not my nature to think or say anything with such conviction. Had I made that prayer up myself, it would have gone something like this, *Dear Jesus, may I please touch your cloak so you might heal me, please?* Not this time. My prayer was not a request. It was fact. I was already touching Jesus' cloak within the Eucharist, and I had no reason to ask permission. I was

---

5 This thought coincided with the story of a woman suffering from hemorrhages for 12 years. She was healed after touching Jesus' cloak, and Jesus told her it was her faith that healed her (Matthew 9:20-22 and Mark 5:25-34). I had not recently read this account in scripture, so I believe the Spirit provided my prayer to Jesus in the Eucharist, including my conviction of faith.

confident – if not commanding. He would heal my old heart. From that day forward, when I approach the altar I ask to be in awe of Jesus. There are times when I don't feel any different, but my heart still recognizes Christ's presence. There are times when I am flooded with awe and thanksgiving for this incredible, physical union with our God.

Growing ever closer to God changed more than just the way I worship. Having a serious relationship with Him reshaped the way I think, pray, work, and interact with others. This positive growth comes down to God's grace helping me become the person I was meant to become as a reflection of Christ. It wasn't that grace did not exist in my lukewarmness, but I didn't recognize it. Once I came to do so, I asked for more and it multiplied. I became wise enough to accept His help and …Voila! I broke out of my self-contained cocoon and took flight.

EYE-OPENER #2: *As a relationship with God deepens, the longing to change goes deeper.*

The transformation into holiness is ongoing. Anything within us that is not befitting of persons made in the image and likeness of God needs to be changed. Besides the obvious, God will bring to the surface things we aren't even aware are holding us back from what He expects. He will grant the grace which allows us to stop anything detrimental to our souls and instead transform us in ways that build us up in holiness. All we need do is sincerely accept it, and in confidence, we will receive the strength, perseverance, and wisdom to cooperate. This grace should be seen as a normal part of living because God will provide everything we need to live as He expects.

A common factor in an ever-developing friendship with God is the desire for continual spiritual growth. The more mature your bond becomes, the stronger the longing for the grace of God. Prayers become more geared toward requesting assistance in becoming ever closer to Him, overcoming shortcomings, growing holier, and better reflecting Christ to others. It becomes more natural to place earthly needs as afterthoughts knowing that God has them covered. I found myself asking God to lead me to being a saint in His eyes (not in a story-about-a-famous-saint way). Most recently, a priest advised me, "Becoming a saint does not happen overnight." Through the power, graces, and miracles of the Holy Spirit, I look forward to the future.

It occurs to me that we are all like Dorothy in Oz.[6] Her friends, the Scarecrow, the Cowardly Lion, and the Tin Man, knew what they wanted changed about themselves, and they went about seeking it. Young Dorothy, having run away from home in disagreement and anger, had to mature to see that her family really did love her, and that she indeed wanted to go home. Her journey to Oz was all about trying to get back to her home in Kansas, but she was seeking help in the wrong direction. As the uncertainties, dangers, and fears of her travels increased, the longing to be home with her loved ones became more intense. In the end, Dorothy was advised by a wiser person that the power to be home was within her all along. All she had to do was face her desire to go home and choose to click her heels three times.

As spiritual Dorothys following the long, winding, yellow brick road of life, we sometimes don't realize that the power to be holy is within us. The Holy Spirit dwells within us as we encounter countless wonders of beauty along with the ugliness of evil. He is with us whether we are feeling high or low at any given moment. It is the power of the Spirit that allows us to recognize what we want changed about ourselves and leads us to seek in the right place – in the hands of God. We only need to stop the noise of life that is

---

6 Lyman Frank Baum, *The Wonderful Wizard of Oz*, (George M. Hill Company: Chicago, 1900)

cupped over our ears singing "la la la la la la" preventing us from discerning the Spirit's direction. Absolutely, we must go about our business of living on Earth. However, if we aim to grow stronger in faith and stay close in relationship with our beloved God, we must click our heels to be at home in a quiet place with Him more often. Otherwise we may find ourselves lost in Oz not realizing that the grace to change has been within us all along just for the choosing.

*G*OD EXPECTS ME
TO DO HIS WILL

Pray then in this way: "Our Father in heaven, hallowed be your name. Your kingdom come. Your will be done, on earth as it is in heaven. (MATTHEW 6:9-10)

I delight to do your will, O my God; your law is within my heart. (PSALM 40:8)

God had my permission to do a total make-over of me. The joy of our relationship had me flying high. The flight pattern was slow and steady, but not plainly laid out in my mind. Even though I had come a long way in prayer life, knowledge of my faith, and in learning to trust Him to assist in this lifelong endeavor, there was still so much to learn. God was prepping to shower another self-awareness blessing upon me. "Your will be done" was a portion of prayer that I hadn't given active consideration outside of Scripture study, but it was beginning to sprout roots that God would water.

EYE-OPENER #1: *God's will includes loving our neighbor.*

What good is it, my brothers and sisters, if you say you have faith but do not have works? Can faith save you? If a brother or sister is naked and lacks daily food, and one of you says to them, "Go in peace, keep warm, and eat your fill," and yet you do not supply their bodily needs, what good is that? So faith by itself, if it has no works, is dead. (JAMES 2:14-17)

You shall love the Lord your God with all your heart, with all your soul, and with all your strength, and with all your mind; and your neighbor as yourself. (LUKE 10:27)

Two, four, six, almost eight years went by since I reintroduced myself to God to ask for my miracle. I read, studied, searched, and absorbed all I could in my endeavor to know God. Right before my eyes, He was granting my request to change and mature within my faith. I was so enthralled with the excitement of growing up in Him, I could have locked myself in a tower somewhere and survived on Scripture and my studies.

Faithfully, I asked the Holy Spirit to guide me in my journey. It was long overdue; an opportunity arose for Him to open my eyes to a shortcoming in my commitment to God. It was one of those "God can pull good from bad" experiences in which I would come to understand that I could no longer bask in Him all by myself. As if I were a little kid sitting at my classroom desk, He was whispering, "pass it on." Wrapped in my thirst for Him, I had the notion that loving God was the easiest thing I'd ever have to do. On the flip side, He was working to get His point across that His command-ments were summed up by two directives: Love God *and* love your neighbor. I was neglecting the second.

It was a tragedy that brought to the surface my need to mature in the "love your neighbor" department. My husband and I lost our home to a fire.

Excuse me for a second while I indulge in a literary cliché:

"It was a dark and stormy night."

Truth be told, it was dark because it was 3:00 a.m. The storm was more of a steady, misty drizzle of rain. Husband and I were sleeping in our upstairs bedroom when we were awakened by the smoke detector. There was no mistaking the shrieking noise. We just weren't sure if it was a false alarm or if it was real. I set a record jumping out of bed to get to the door. Upon opening it, my nose was hit with the odor of smoke mixed with a strong chemical concoction. I turned to Husband and shook my head a violent "yes" signaling the urgency. He vaulted out of bed and down the stairs to locate the source of the fire. It was in the garage. We had a 1970 Mustang convertible hooked up to a battery charger. The charger malfunctioned, overheated, and ignited the fire. Our garage was full of all sorts of treats to feed any fire's appetite. The flames multiplied rapidly.

I dialed 911. Meanwhile, Husband instinctively tried to save our home by sword fighting the blaze with a $29 garden hose minus the missing nozzle. He no longer looked human as adrenaline raged through his veins. I actually saw "The Incredible Hulk" creature in his face as fear and instinct ruled his actions. The battle was futile, but Husband persevered until two policemen arrived and pulled him away to accompany me on the curb.

The adrenaline rush was waning as the chill of the morning reminded my husband that he was in his bare feet wearing only a pair of shorts and a T-shirt. The two of us walked back and forth in the rain as the flames grew in proportion before the fire trucks arrived. While pacing, I sought the comfort of the "Hail Mary" prayer, and I prayed it non-stop because my shocked mind couldn't pull anything else up. Everything would be OK. In an unusual calm for the circumstance, I knew this was true. I remember looking up into the clouds and whispering to God that I was confident He would culture good out of this crisis. That's the way He works. I asked Him to help me see the good part as soon as possible.

As the house burned and firefighters fought, neighbors from across the street herded us in for hot coffee. We made phone calls from their kitchen including one to our insurance agent, who quickly arrived on the scene. He handed us an emergency check to purchase provisions that might offer some normalcy in the days ahead. First stop Kmart. After picking out what we saw as bare necessities, we headed for the cashier. She rang up our toothpaste, toothbrushes, combs, deodorant, socks, underwear, sweats, and a few more miscellaneous items. The price tag for basic essentials added up to $75. Husband looked at me and I looked at him. We needed no words. Our eyes conveyed how fortunate we were to have insurance. Otherwise, we would not have taken the luxury of shopping at Kmart the same day the house burned down.

The two of us were different after the fire. Technically we were homeless and stripped of earthly treasures, yet thankful to be alive. We were dependent on the charity of others through that very long first day. It was a strong life lesson to have virtually nothing.

The world was different after the fire. People at work were sending cards and leaving messages that they were praying for us. Previous to the fire, most work people didn't talk about God. Now He was out in the open.

He tells us in Scripture that He will provide, and that there is no need to worry about food and clothing:

Therefore I tell you, do not worry about your life, what you will eat or what you will drink, or about your body, what you will wear. Is not life more than food, and the body more than clothing? Look at the birds of the air; they neither sow nor reap nor gather into barns, and yet your heavenly Father feeds them. Are you not of more value than they?...But if God so clothes the grass of the field, which is alive today and tomorrow is thrown into the oven, will he not much more clothe you – you of little faith? (MATTHEW 6:25-30)

It was happening. In the days following, so many people coordinated efforts to help with our immediate needs. Family, neighbors, friends, co-workers, and strangers were providing us with food, water, clothing, and shelter. The insurance provisions allowed us to move into a nearby hotel by the end of that first evening. After sorting through the remains of the house, one neighbor let us use their shower so we didn't have to drive back to the hotel in puffs of soot. A few weeks later, Dave and Sue next door arranged to have us move into a vacant house owned by their family, which was being prepared for the market. It wasn't our own, but this temporary lodging was such a luxury compared to living in the cramped hotel efficiency. Our friend, Joanie, delivered a huge pan of pasta the day we settled into the house, and we didn't have to worry about planning dinner for a couple days. A dear friend from work, Christine, went shopping on her lunch hour after hearing about the fire. She was not shopping for herself, but was buying bath towels we hadn't remembered and blouses I could wear to the office. On her way home from work she stopped by to drop off her purchases. A few days later, Christine arrived to help sort through the mess inside our home. Her kindheartedness is always on automatic pilot. She never waits around to be invited to help, but instead goes about doing what needs doing. It had been years since I saw a former co-worker, Beth, but when she heard about the situation, she showed up on our charred doorstep ready for cleanup duty. I will always treasure the gift she gave with her unannounced presence.

Perhaps I was touched most by the inborn kindness offered by my niece, May, who was four and a half years old at the time. On a visit to my sister's home after the fire, May was sitting beside her mom, Rebecca, taking in the conversation around her. Aware that her Uncle and I had lost our possessions, she disappeared from the room momentarily and reappeared with a gift. She gave me a little cardboard sheet displaying 20 pair of brand new, shiny, stick-on earrings of varying colors and shapes for my unadorned ear lobes. I proudly wore my new jewelry until the sticky stuff on each and every pair would no longer adhere to my skin. Compassion need not be complicated.

I must stop with the list, but there were many others who reached out to us until we were situated back in our rebuilt home.

This interruption of our lives allowed the blinders to fall off for both of us. We realized how much we took for granted, how much we had together, and how much we didn't need. God's people teach by example. I saw the generous, loving, compassionate faces of so many of them.

Compassion! That's what was missing. Somewhere along the way while tending to my career and educational ambitions, I lost my ability to feel compassion. I was apathetic toward other people's situations or needs. If it didn't involve me or my family, I didn't need to be concerned. Somebody at work would be affected by a personal or family difficulty, but I didn't see it. Every evening on the news I heard about murder, rape, house fires, catastrophes, and chaos, but I had learned to tune out. God caught my attention in the fire aftermath and gave my sight and hearing back. Through receiving, I learned about giving. Born from compassion, the active gift of love was being poured out on Husband and me. I began seeing the example of others in a different light. It was the light of the Lord. The question became how one goes about becoming compassionate. Awareness is the first step toward change. I asked God to help me acquire this virtue.

God was molding me within the experiences of life. The next few lessons would bring out a deeper meaning of those prayerful words "Your will be done" to include loving others.

EYE-OPENER #2:   *God's whisper, the Holy Spirit, is the gift that prompts us into action.*

Teach me to do your will, for you are my God. Let your good spirit lead me on a level path. (PSALM 143:10)

Within a week after the fire, Husband and I returned to work. The corporate pace was a stabilizer while we waited for our house to be rebuilt. Close to a year later, we returned home to a yet unfinished house. Even so, moving back was a joy and a triumph. It became a blessing in a new, emotional, spiritual way that is hard to describe. We took nothing for granted. We gained a keen awareness of the differences between luxuries and necessities and between wants and needs.

Once back to work, I fell into my schedule of getting to church during lunch hours. The day was not complete without that visit. My time with the Lord was one of the cozy perks of being employed in a building just across the street. Perhaps it was the only perk that mattered.

Daily prayers included a request to succeed at moving up in my career. I had been in my current position almost five years. It was time for a change. The wind was right. Both the general manager and my supervisor were supporting my efforts to be promoted out of the department into another area. After acquiring experience elsewhere, I hoped to be promoted back within that same department in the future. I worked diligently in my duties, all the while watching postings for internal job openings. Over a two-year time span, I applied for almost a dozen positions. It was a big company with many qualified employees in the mix. Interviewing in different departments was a good way to network in diverse areas. I applied regularly, interviewed periodically, and was turned down methodically. The managers who conducted the interviews provided good feedback. Somehow, I always came close, but never got the cigar. I was not discouraged. This was part of corporate life. I kept trying. I kept praying.

The perfect opening finally hit the postings within a department where I previously worked for over 10 years. I could return with more experience, maturity, and business sense. Every day during the two-week wait after my interview, I went to church and included a request for this perfect job. Things were looking good. My bosses were under the impression that I was the frontrunner according to the interviewing manager. A formal offer had not been made, but my superiors didn't want to delay listing my soon-to-be-vacant seat in order to avoid my leaving before training a new person. Things looked so positive that the department managers posted my job as being open before I was officially hired by the new department. It made quite a stir since it had not been announced that I accepted any offer. Murphy's Law kicked in. A qualified candidate, whose current position was to be eliminated, applied at the last minute, was interviewed, and hired.

That turndown finally broke my spirit. I stormed over to church and vented my anger to God. What did He want from me? Obviously, motherhood was not in my cards, so why not further my career? I stormed back to work. I was not at peace. I wanted that job. In other words, "my will be done."

Despite the disappointment, I continued my lunch time vigils. I apologized to God for my temper tantrum and proceeded to pray in a "Your will be done" fashion. I meant it, but I felt I didn't understand God's voice because I didn't know where my future was going. On second thought, to be perfectly honest, all the while I was job searching, I brushed aside the whispers within me. That soft voice had a conflicting tone to it.

There are always two sides to every story. For years, I rolled with the version that I wanted to progress as a professional in the corporate environment. With no children to juggle my career against, I must be meant to move on and up, earn a nice pension, retire early, and enjoy the golden years with my husband. Much of this first story line was true because there was a lot I liked about my job. Even so, I began to struggle with a second adaptation of the saga. Every time the alternate theme reared its ugly head, I pushed it back down and ignored it. It posed the question as to whether I sincerely wanted to continue in the corporate environment or not.

If the second version were a movie, it would portray me as having a high level of anxiety at work. I would have dutifully argued with the screen writers that their portrayal was incorrect. Out of habit, I would have presented the aura that I loved everything about corporate life. My alter ego in the screen play was trying desperately to advance in her career, the only way of life familiar to her. Secretly she had grown unhappy. Sure she was helping the corporation feed its bottom line, but that wasn't really fulfilling to her in the way society markets it.

Well into this hypothetical film, Story Line Two would have me leaving work every evening later than planned. I would drive home worrying about rushing to pull a quick dinner together. Upon entering the door, I braced for a cold welcome because I neglected to call and mention I'd be late - *again*. The weekends were not relaxing either. There were errands, chores, and grocery shopping to catch up on. I squeezed my parents in when they needed me and saw my mother-in-law on holidays. My nieces and nephews rarely set eyes on me, so they couldn't see the "aunt" in me. There would be no happy ending running full throttle seven days a week in order to meet the current, cultural definition of success.

The movie audience would sympathize with my character as

visions of insignificance danced in her head. Deep down she knew there was more to life, something deeper, something more to be done besides fill a position that could be filled by someone else — something perhaps her increasing faith was drawing her toward. The tension would hang in the air and leave the alternative endings to be determined in the sequel.

Working for a living is a noble and necessary task. I am very grateful for the years spent in the workforce because I gained a wealth of experience, education, and travel. However, for me, my career had become a burden and a detour from bringing forth the gifts God knit within me. When cultivated and used, these gifts would allow me to grow into my "me" shoes, those of the unique person I was born to be by God's loving design. The nagging voice from within was moving me in a direction to quit work and follow the story line that would land on the love-thy-neighbor side of life. It seemed time to mesh the valuable growth I had undergone in the corporate setting and put it to good use on a different level.

After allowing time to contemplate these conflicting paths, the desire to quit became loud and clear. I acknowledged the possibility that this might be something God was whispering. I went to Him for wisdom in this huge decision. *OK, Lord. Help me figure this out. I'm anxious. How do I know if I should take such a drastic step? Lead me to the peace, please. If leaving my job is not the right path, please put a roadblock in my way.* With prayers said, my plan was to quit working unless something interfered.

I had choked down that whisper to abandon my career for way too long without confiding in Husband. It was coming up on the 2000 Christmas season. Husband and I would have the week between Christmas and New Year's Day to relax and focus on each other. Procrastination for another few weeks wouldn't hurt. If I was lucky, the ridiculous idea of quitting would go away.

I thought for sure my husband would present the roadblock. It was only logical that he would ask me to wait a year or two, give it more thought, or ask for a sabbatical before burning any bridges. The reaction I expected was the only one that made sense.

It was time. "Husband, we need to talk." Those words made him nervous because it meant something serious was in the air. He turned the TV off and tuned into me. While pacing, I told him of my inclination to quit work; there must be other things meant for me to pursue. What he was hearing came from left field. He never saw it coming. He listened intently and waited until I finished before saying anything.

There. It was out. I waited for a rebuttal. Instead Husband said, "We can do this." He grabbed a paper and pen. We began calculating a new budget to put in place after deleting my salary from the coffers. I left the corporate workforce with peace and confidence that it was the direction to follow.

Amidst the process of deciding to "retire," waiting a couple months to give notice, then working toward my final day, I was experiencing another nagging. A strong desire developed to volunteer with the elderly. I also gained an emotional longing to work with teenagers who didn't know God personally. You could say God was granting my request for the compassion I couldn't produce on my own. He was dousing me with heart strings, which pulled me toward these two sets of people. The desire to work with the elderly was understandable. The aspiration to work with teenagers was an absolute mystery. Until that point, I had a discomfort with teens in general despite the fact I used to be one. Surely, I could not relate to that segment of the population even if I tried. It seemed overnight my heart melted. Once unemployed, my extracurricular activities included volunteer work with both the elderly and God's adolescent children.

God's timing is perfect. After studying Scripture on my own for close to a decade, there was now the time to share Him in a more specific way. I began experiencing that familiar bubbling up feeling. Something was brewing. That "bubbling up" is the way God pushes me into action. Otherwise, I tend to bury my thoughts when they involve going off in unfamiliar territory. He understands my personality better than I do, and He counteracts my hesitancy by pushing the thoughts back up to the surface until I cannot contain them anymore. The energy and excitement about everything I learned through Scripture forced me to act. I called our parish's Outreach Director, Owen, to find out how I might put this love for Scripture to good use. We had a long conversation as I explained this wish to share God's Word. I also conveyed my lack of understanding as to why, after 10 years, I felt compelled to make this move. He simply stated, "God's telling you that you're ready."

The Director's encouragement prompted me to contact the Youth Minister at our church. We arranged for me to lead a summer Bible study with the high school students. Father Joe had just been assigned as our new pastor. One evening on my way to meet with the teens, I took the opportunity to introduce myself as we passed in the hallway. He thanked me for volunteering my time. In response, I told Father that I loved sharing Scripture, and I was glad to do so, but I didn't feel a real need here. Those attending the summer Bible study were already in love with the Lord. Explaining further, I told him that my heart was hurting for teens who didn't know God. Oh, did that hit a high note for Father; he had just the thing. At his previous parish, he was also the chaplain for the nearby Youth Development Center (YDC). The YDC was a maximum security prison housing adolescent males sentenced by the State to serve time for crimes committed. Father's heart still belonged to those teens. He missed his ministry there, but he was called to new duties. He suggested that I consider sharing Christ with these young men. In so many words, "no" was my answer. I couldn't see myself working amidst hardened criminals. It would be too uncomfortable. He understood. I went on my merry way to meet up with more saintly teens just down the hall.

Self-nagging is difficult to ignore. My mind would not stop turning over Father Joe's suggestion. Maybe it was in me to work with young criminals. Maybe I'm supposed to do this. After all, I wanted to work with teens who didn't know God. The boys at YDC surely fit that description. I called Father to tell him that I'd like to try after all. In a subsequent conversation with him, I remember saying that I didn't know if this was from God or not. He quietly replied, "It's from God" as he lightly nodded his head. He knew what I have since learned. If my heart is considering an action that glorifies God and is in line with His command to love Him and our neighbor, then that is the influence of the Spirit. This nagging was a lesson in discerning His promptings.

Father put me back in touch with Owen, and the three of us began planning. A door was then open for developing a Bible study program for teens who didn't know God well at all.

Just prior to the Bible study launch, I was invited to participate in a spiritual retreat weekend at the prison. This "Metanoia" (Greek: Change of heart) event was sponsored by Father's previous parish. This would be a great opportunity to meet the teens and be coached by veteran volunteers who coordinated retreats at YDC. As the weekend approached, I was getting cold feet wondering if I had anything to offer these delinquent kids. The amiable side of me did not lend itself easily to conflict, and I feared being intimidated by the inmates rather than being able to teach them. I was getting more nervous by the day. I kept telling God, there must be a mistake. Surely, He could see that I was not the right person for the job.

Something was bound to happen that would stop me from taking part. Something never happened.

From the minute I met the boys on the first evening of the retreat, I felt totally at peace. This was it. This is what I wanted to do. Father Joe was right; it was God's grace that led me where He wanted me to be at this moment in time.

EYE-OPENER #3:   *God's will includes sharing our talents for the building up of others.*

> *For as in one body we have many members, and not all the members have the same function, so we, who are many, are one body in Christ, and individually we are members one of another. We have gifts that differ according to the grace given to us: prophecy, in proportion to faith; ministry, in minister-ing; the teacher, in teaching; the exhorter, in exhortation; the giver, in generosity; the leader, in diligence; the compassionate, with cheerfulness.* (ROMANS 12:4-8)

Each individual is gifted with inborn, designer talents and potential. The Designer is God. He promotes those talents with His grace, which includes guidance from other people we encounter who are also gifted. Hopefully, His grace moves each person to ac-knowledge and nurture his or her own gifts. Those abilities, in turn, bear good fruit when we share them for the building up of others for the glory of God.

It is wise to acknowledge that we are talented not of our own making, but through the grace of God:

> *For by the grace given to me I say to everyone among you not to think of yourself more highly than you ought to think, but*

to think with sober judgment, each according to the measure of faith that God has assigned. (ROMANS 12:3)

Looking back several years before leaving the work field, there was one job promotion that forced me to enter into the world of public speaking. Talking in front of a crowd was not a talent I ever intended to nurture. Instead, it was a mental and physical ordeal for me. Fifteen minutes prior to curtain time, I would have severe stomach cramps that sent me rushing to the nearest restroom. Shortly after beginning a presentation, the number of people staring at me would sink in. Then my voice would shake and crack and my mind could not focus, which all made it impossible to conceal that I was very nervous. Nevertheless, presentations became part of my duties. In my new role, I was scheduled to conduct a seminar in front of about 50 people. I accepted the burden without giving a clue about my fear and dedicated myself to doing the best I could possibly do. I practiced for hours and days. Playtime was over, and it was time to pack my clothes, my briefcase, and fly to California for my debut. The day before the trip, I made especially sure I spent my lunch hour in church. I attended Mass and stayed afterward to say the rosary. My last 10 minutes before going back to work were spent crying to the Blessed Mother, *I can't do this, please ask God to cancel my trip. I just can't do this.* The next morning, I was on the plane practicing my presentation. In case she didn't hear me the first time, that night in my hotel room, I beseeched the Blessed Mother to do something quick. I prayed the rosary before falling asleep.

Fifteen minutes before the seminar, I was in the Ladies' Room and not surprised by the need. The surprise came during my speech. I was calm, pleasant, and confident for the entire hour of talking. Anyone who has experienced anxiety speaking in public will vouch that this could be nothing short of miraculous. Many times since that first major speaking task, I have thanked God for the grace to overcome a fear that I would have never voluntarily faced.

It was in 2002 while developing the program at YDC that my quasi-talent of speaking in front of a group came in handy. First, informational meetings were necessary to request support from the people in charge at the center. Then a kick-off event was held to launch the program and generate attendance. With the clout of Father Joe at YDC, and with the Outreach Director as my right hand, we pulled it together.

Approximately 25 teens showed up for the initial presentation, plus various YDC staff members, security guards, and volunteers from our parish. The gathering was to begin with the Lord's Prayer. Anticipating that many of the boys were not familiar with the words, I prepared a poster board displaying the prayer in very large, bold lettering. With the poster board held high, we lifted our voices in unity and prayed the Lord's Prayer.

The kick-off sparked interest, and the Bible Study was up and running successfully. Attendance slowly grew, and the class evolved as I became more confident in my task as both teacher and preacher. The program could not have been initiated without the assistance of Father Joe, Owen, and the staff at YDC. My deepest gratitude also goes to Sister Yvonne who was a religious liaison to the boys at the facility. At the end of her work day, she voluntarily stayed to sit in on each Wednesday evening discussion. She let me bounce many an idea off her to guide me with my lesson plans. The teens made it a success as well. They showed up. Some of them came despite negative pressure from peers who didn't think God was cool. Not only did the students learn, but they taught me about what God puts in each of us from the time we are conceived. If we cooperate, God brings out the best in a person that lies buried under layers of hurt, defensiveness, misinformation, stubbornness, and ego.

As the YDC program progressed, I was asked to speak before the parish congregation about it. The parishioners knew of Father Joe's passion for these wayward boys, and my purpose was to extend an invitation for people to become involved. The request was made for letters to be written to the teens attending an upcoming Metanoia retreat. First names of the attendees were listed in the bulletin asking families to write a spiritually inspiring and supportive note to a boy on the list. These notes would be distributed during the retreat. The response was wonderful. These letters often bring tears to the boys' eyes as they experience God's love through others, a side of people they don't often come across.

On another occasion, I spoke at a parish Family Religious Education class. With the approach of the feast of the Epiphany, the theme for that particular session was "Finding Jesus in Unlikely Places." The Epiphany commemorates when the three wise men from afar met Jesus as a baby (Matthew 2:1-12). The Religious Education Director asked that I talk about this Scriptural event in relation to my work at YDC. These men were astronomers who followed a star in search of the new ruler prophesized in Scripture. They found Him, but it was totally unexpected for the search to end with a poor infant born in a manger. It may be unexpected as well, but if time was taken to search, Jesus could be found in each of the boys confined at the juvenile prison. He's waiting to bubble over so that each cannot help but notice Him and someday expect Him to be their God. At the end of class, parents and students were asked to spiritually adopt a YDC teen and commit to praying for him for at least one year. The families enthusiastically participated.

EYE-OPENER #4:   *God will provide the means to get done what He wants done.*

And the good news must first be proclaimed to all nations. When they bring you to trial and hand you over, do not worry beforehand about what you are to say; but say whatever is given you at that time, for it is not you who are speaking, but the Holy Spirit. (MARK 13:10-11)

It was volunteering at the YDC that brought me to truly believe that if God wants something done by someone, He will provide the talent and means to get it done through that individual or with the assistance of others.

Although the Bible study was running and making progress, I often questioned if I was up to the task. With this lack of confidence, I ran to God with an invitation every week to help me do a good job. Prayer came easily. I was attending Mass prior to each session, stopping before the Tabernacle to make a plea for a great class, and constantly asking the Holy Spirit to guide me in preparing and conducting classes and to guide those participating. Unfortunately, these prayerful habits developed into a bit of a problem. I became anxious that if I didn't stop to pray enough or visit church, I would sabotage the class and fail. It was as if I pictured God standing around doing nothing until I forced His hand by praying sufficiently. At this point in my spiritual development, I had drawn closer to Christ and trusted His Spirit to inspire me. However, remnants remained of my image of God the Father being the stern disciplinarian standing by only to correct any slip ups. What a relief when I became confident that He was helping me even if I didn't make it to church that day. I had already given my heart over to Him in my efforts to share Him with the students. My actions themselves became prayer. God gave me the grace to use my passion for His Word to teach these teens. It was a fact that no matter how many prayers I sent above, each boy had to make their own choice in the matter. Prayer can soften hearts, but each teen still had the final say. They had to choose to show up, choose to ignore the harassment from peers, and choose to behave and participate once they were in class. I poured myself into preparation before class, but was not able to predict the response of those attending. Praying, stopping at church, or going to Mass were for my own peace, strength, and growth as I encountered each day, and not a prerequisite or guarantee of having a good class. No matter what the outcome, I learned to see God at work, and grew to trust that He was with me on the bad days as well as the good.

Each individual at YDC had a story. Most of the life stories were void of any awareness of God working in their lives, but I could see Him underneath it all. Buried within each criminal mind, stripped of the anger, the confusion, the hardness, and the mask, was a child of God. Each was a unique personality worth uncovering. One such personality was Carl. He belonged to a gang and was a rather husky young man about 17 years old. He attended one of the weekend retreats where I participated as a speaker. I was assigned as leader of one of the tables to guide small group discussions throughout the program. Carl was seated at my table along with several other teens. Layers of hardness of heart would peel away from these guys over several days spent listening and sharing at the retreat sessions. On Sunday before the program ended, the adult leaders accompanied the boys from their table to the chapel for Eucharistic Adoration. Each group would have a 15 minute visit in the chapel. Most of them had no idea what Eucharistic Adoration entailed, but they heard a brief summary on this prayer practice from a priest during the workshop segment. It did not matter if they did not understand because Christ understood each of them.

Within this paragraph I give you my layman's explanation of Eucharistic Adoration. This devotion is based on the Catholic conviction that Jesus becomes physically present when the priest consecrates the bread and wine at Holy Mass. Parishioners receive the body and blood of Jesus under the auspices of bread and wine. This transformation of species is called Transubstantiation. It is an amazing phenomenon to grasp because it is not natural, but supernatural. Faith in our supernatural God allows us to know that nothing is impossible through Him. The Eucharist is the center of Catholicism. Faith in the true presence of Christ in the Eucharist traces back to Christ's directives to the Apostles. As time went by, the Church sanctioned adoration of Jesus in the Eucharist at times other than at Mass. Cloaked as a host of bread, Christ is universally, physically present in the Tabernacle of every Catholic Church. A candle burns non-stop beside the Tabernacle to announce His constant presence. It is here that individuals can spend time with Christ in the peace and quiet of a loving, strengthening, perfect friendship in every sense of the word.

Carl was in the group I took to the chapel. We only had 15 minutes in front of our Lord before the next group arrived and we would take our leave. Because I didn't think trying to explain Adoration of Jesus in "a piece of bread" in such a small time frame was realistic, the plan was to let these young men sit in silent prayer during the time allotted. It didn't happen that way. I recall getting up from my chair and confidently announcing that they were in the presence of Jesus. Now was the time to let loose in silent prayer about every hurt and burden they've been carrying around. Now was the time to ask for strength to change what needs to be changed in their lives. Now was the time to drop everything inside of them at the foot of our Lord's cross and leave it there for Him to help with always. My words were not prepared ahead of time, but came out so quickly and precisely that it had to be the Holy Spirit leading. The last half of our chapel time was spent in silence. As we left the building each boy was crying. He had touched them.

It came time to say goodbye to Carl. With a hardy handshake, I told him I loved him. He burst into tears. Carl softly replied that no one ever told him that before. He knew as well as I did it was the love of God.

Like most of the young men at YDC, Carl served his time and was once again given his freedom. If they qualify, and if their city has the funding, some go on to educational, or work programs. Carl's heart was heavy the last time I saw him because he had felt the love of God and wanted more of it. Unfortunately, he was sent back to his neighborhood where he lived with his drug-addicted sister in the middle of gang land. There is no follow-up on the success of each teen after release from prison, but Carl's chances of relapsing into crime and drugs were high based on his environment. Odds were against him. There were as many crack houses on the corners as there were churches. His parole requirements forbid entering the vicinity of a drug holdout, so this meant that going to a neighborhood church would breach parole. We must pray, pray, and pray for Carl and the too many souls like him that they might learn to trust in God's presence to get them through the worst of times.

Personalities would come and go over my tenure of two and a half years at the YDC. My devotion to research, prepare, and spend an hour each week with these troubled teens never waned. I wanted nothing more than to share the Trinity with them. Although I left each session feeling totally drained, the joy I felt on the drive home was uplifting. I thanked God for the incredible experience of sharing Him and for the awareness that I had taken on something I would not have done apart from Him. He was driving me and putting to use energy and skills that I didn't know I possessed. I was a willing vehicle and He used me fruitfully. This was not "the me" I knew, but it was "the me" who God knew. Inspired by the Spirit, I understood that nothing is impossible with God.

Although public speaking abilities came out of necessity, the enjoyment I receive from writing on varying subjects has always naturally pulled me toward this skill. I compose poems about anything from my favorite ice cream, to a birthday message coded in baseball lingo for capturing my husband's heart, to a rhyme about my dog, to personal ditties on Christmas cards. Nieces and nephews tease me because I don't just send birthday greetings; I write "books" inside the cards. Simply put, I love to write.

Many moons ago prior to conceiving the idea of a book, I knelt before the Tabernacle to talk to the Lord about my penchant for writing. With many thanks for this gift, this joy, this passion, I expressed the desire to put down on paper what He has done in my life, hoping to inspire others to draw closer to Him. With confidence, I gave myself to Him and asked for the grace and guidance to do so. Not long after that chat, a photo flash appeared in my mind's eye. It was a white paperback book with big, black, bold letters written diagonally across the cover. The letters read, GOD EXPECTS ME. With this title in mind, I began writing in 2005.

Several years into the project, I began struggling with doubts that God was blessing my writing efforts. On one of my trips to church to sit alone with the Lord, I prayed about these doubts and frustrations. *Please let me hear what You have to say, Lord. Is Your Father working with me on this, or am I writing for myself? I don't want this for my own satisfaction, but to help others come to know the Father, Son, and Holy Spirit. Am I spending so much time on the computer and spinning my wheels for my own ambitions?*

It is difficult for me to stop to listen in silence, allowing grace from above to fall upon the ears of my heart and mind. So, I prayed some more. *Help me quiet my mind. Help me to listen, to discern.* I was churning right in front of our Lord in the Tabernacle. I tried to relax as I began to breathe in slowly and deeply a few times. The next thought that came my way was: *Talent is a gift from God, but in itself is not enough. The gift must be offered back to God and then it will become what He allows.*

I smiled. I was peaceful. I continued to pray and write.

EYE-OPENER #5:   *A groundbreaking prayer: "Lord, I give You my will."*

The process of maturing spiritually led me to pray that I would do His will, not mine. Daily, I begged, if not demanded, that He tell me what His plan for me was so I could run with it. After years of frustration thinking God was so silent on the matter, I came to realize my avid desire to do His will was well intended, but still evolving.

It was while launching the Bible study at the YDC that I put my experience with God's will into words. To catch the interest of these young men, I introduced God's will by describing it as a football. I asked them to picture God as the Head Coach with all humans as players on His team on Earth. As Coach, He guides each player in an appropriate position to highlight talents that will benefit the team as a whole. Some of us have our arms wide open to receive the ball. If the ball is thrown off to the side, we are willing to change directions to catch it. Christ's own mother, Mary, is a firm example of one who willingly changed her path in life to obey God's bidding. Then there are those who aren't so sure He knows what He's talking about. Take for example John the Baptist's father, Zechariah. He was a very faithful, holy man serving as a high priest in the temple, but he doubted God's game plan. Coach God sent an angel onto the field to pass a message directly to Zechariah. The angel shared God's strategy that the high priest and his wife would conceive a son even though they were very old. Imagine this big-time player folding his arms in disbelief that the football would ever make it to him. He let the ball drop in front of him. After sitting on the penalty bench for a bit, Zechariah had a change of heart and believed in the wisdom of his Coach. There are also some who are not in it for the team, and management would consider sewing the nickname "hotdogger" on their jerseys. That was me. My arms were held wide open to catch the football. There I stood coaching God to pass me the ball, let me catch it, and then get out of my way so I could run off in my own direction. There was an arrogant tone to my prayers, *Come on, God, pass me the ball. Come on, over here. Not that way, Lord, this way.* I wanted to do His will, but subconsciously expected His desires to be mine. I was telling the Creator of Heaven and Earth what to do. It was a bad habit.

It was during one ordinary visit to the Tabernacle when my tone changed. I sat in a pew silently praying that I would do what God wanted. This particular day, the prayer took a twist. Instead of praying, *Lord, let me know Your will,* my words said, *I give You my will.* As soon as that sentiment was uttered within my mind, I giggled. It finally dawned on me that I must give up my predetermined will in order to be at peace with His. Trusting that God has a handle on things, even if they are not what I expect, allows me to accept His will as mine.

It was not long after that hit-myself-on-the-forehead and say "duh" moment that I consciously changed another prayer. I told God that I was tired. My husband was tired. We were emotionally drained from praying and hoping for a baby. Friends were telling us to not try so hard, to not think about it so much, and then we'd get pregnant. I explained my frustration to God, *Lord, how can I not think about it when you created my body to remind me when I can get pregnant, when I cannot, and when I am not. How could my spouse not think about it when he secretly counted my days to fertility?* My prayers turned into a request for peace for both of us if we would not be graced with a baby. It was a "Thy will be done" prayer. Peace came quickly after the request was made. We quit counting.

With age comes wisdom. The answer was "no" to years of pregnancy requests. That "no" was accompanied by the peace to accept it. Today, I understand that God squeezed good out of that disappointment in more ways than one. Praying for a baby was a path to a more mature prayer life, and it led me to further my education in faith matters. I grew up spiritually and embraced my personal God. Had I been caring for my own children, it is doubtful I would have taken time to reach out to troubled teens. It was the challenge of the YDC Bible study that first brought me to comprehend the reality that nothing is impossible with God. It was also the turning point where I began to exercise gifts that God had knit into me for the building up of the Body of Christ.

EYE-OPENER #6: *Sometimes we are forced by circumstance to discover talents.*

Talent does not need to be defined in an artistic way. Talent can be anything a person wants to share with others such as: sharing time, finances, conversation, or wisdom, being a good listener, a good example, a care giver, or a mentor, or an offering of any number of gifts. All are as good as gold.

We discover talents in varying ways. Early on in life, parents and mentors begin the process of bringing out our strengths. We develop these abilities further, and discover new ones, by attending school, trying new things, taking advanced classes, and sometimes by surprise. There are also times when we discover our talents through need.

While on one of my morning walks with God, I pondered circumstance being the impetus that helps develop skills. That sunny day, I focused on Christ making His way to Calvary to die. My mind saw a tortured Jesus struggling to carry the cross. God responded to His Son's immediate needs in the form of Simon of Cyrene. Simon was seized from the crowd by Roman soldiers and forced to carry the cross for Jesus who was near death:

As they led him away, they seized a man, Simon of Cyrene, who was coming from the country, and they laid the cross on him, and made him carry it behind Jesus. (LUKE 23:26)

This man did not volunteer to assist God's Son, but rather was commissioned into service. Scripture does not tell us much about Simon. My guess is that he would have been quite stressed after being grabbed by the soldiers. Perhaps he feared for his life while being pushed into the path of wrath against the condemned Jesus. Maybe he was pulled out of the crowd because he had bulging muscles and was strong enough to carry the cross. Even though Simon was forced to help, the end result was that help was given. He used all his might to carry the cross of Christ. Albeit forcefully, it was still a fact that Simon served his neighbor. I believe God would have graced him through his painful experience in a way that would change him forever for the good.

Situations arise in which we joyfully rush to the side of someone in need much like Mary did when elderly Elizabeth was six months pregnant. Conversely, we encounter circumstances that blindside us into action like Simon, but yet we face these trials with all of our muscle. My husband and I became Simons for each other during our trials with infertility and the house fire. Other instances that come to mind are: illness, loss of employment, troubled relationships, death of loved ones, and financial difficulties. Being commissioned has advantages. It moves us to tackle change instead of avoiding it for the sake of a more comfortable routine. Commissioning is different than volunteering in that it is usually a service of immediate need for a close relative or friend. It may draw you in before you are aware of what is happening. Often you roll with the punches instead of having the freedom volunteering might allow for picking and choosing who, when, and where to help. In the end, we become better, stronger Simons from our challenges.

Mrs. C is a long-time family friend who comes to mind as a prime example of a Simon. Her son, David, was born with Cerebral Palsy in the late sixties and raised during an era that did not fare well for the physically challenged. Mrs. C and her husband prayed non-stop for strength and guidance to do what was best for their child. Knowing nothing about where to begin, she claims it was the grace of God that strengthened and empowered her to pursue her son's best interests and education. As she was commissioned into service for her family's sake, she mustard up all of her abilities to do what she needed to do. Her continuous efforts allowed David to achieve his goal of independence and to live productively in a world that would have written him off from day one. After confronting the obstacles in the midst of David's debilitating disease, this Mom of faith went on to become a pioneer in opening doors to other people with physical challenges. In the early seventies, she was instrumental in guiding my parents to push for academic help for my sister, Jean, who struggled with dyslexia-induced disabilities and she stuttered. Learning disabilities were not diagnosed in the seventies, and students having these types of issues were categorized as trouble makers, lazy, or slow. These children were being pushed aside and lost academically because they couldn't keep up with the one-size-fits-all teaching mold. Mrs. C challenged this concept and became Jean's advocate. The school district insisted that my sister was the only child in need of help, and the budget did not allow for a class for one teen. Mrs. C began her mission to prove that this was not a one student issue. A political battle ensued, but ended as she brought forward enough students with similar disabilities to justify a class. A specialized class was finally installed when Jean was a senior. She was tested and diagnosed with dyslexia, which explained why she had such difficulty with reading and math. She was given assistance in learning to conquer dyslexia and her speech issues. The program was a success. Special programs are now standard in schools because the number of children with special needs has never dwindled. Those years of struggling to make progress socially for the disabled prompted Mrs. C to become a professional advocate for those who don't know where to begin. Being forced so long ago to be a Simon turned into a dedication to help others avoid those same barriers. This woman put her many talents to use in the service of others. She is proof that whatever adversity life brings, God will allow good to develop from it – if we become His willing instruments.

Six years ago, Husband and I became Simons for his mother, Carmella, who was diagnosed with breast cancer. The initial reaction to her diagnosis was fear of the unknown. The three of us found support in one another to take things a day at a time, but head on. We also had confidence that God would accompany us as we took steps toward unfamiliar territory. He responded to our needs by sending an angel in the form of Carmella's next door neighbor, Mrs. L, a retired nurse. The skills and knowledge she shared about breast cancer took much of the anxiety away. Mrs. L unmasked the mystery, which made it easier for our family to understand what came next regarding surgery and treatment.

As longevity has increased with medical technology, it is common for adults to be commissioned to assist parents who are well into their golden years. Husband's mother was a very independent woman until just a couple years ago when she began requiring more TLC than she ever wanted. She had come through her cancer experience with flying colors, but increasingly became more tired, frail, and confused. Through it all she kept both her humor and her stubbornness. One of the amusing stories stemming from her stubbornness presented itself during a follow-up doctor appointment. Carmella had been taking an estrogen blocker to prevent the tumor from reoccurring. She was not at all happy about having to take a prescription pill over a five year span, but she complied with the doctor's wishes. As her Simon, I escorted her to follow-up appointments with her doctor. We sat in the waiting room prior to one appointment and carried on conversation, which people seated nearby could hear without strain. Jumping from one topic to the next, Carmella announced she was thinking about "getting off the pill." The laugh inside my belly had to be subdued. I wasn't sure if it was best to ignore the connotation of her comment, or if I should tell her to keep her voice down before the men in the room began to introduce themselves. God rest her soul, Carmella was 89 when she passed away in 2014.

My own mother is beginning to have more than her share of health issues and doctor appointments. Mom lives with two of my sisters, her Simons right now. The rest of us pitch in to coordinate rides, cook meals, and do what needs to be done. Thankfully, along with her own stubbornness, she has a quick-witted humor that keeps her ailments from getting the best of her. Because of diabetes, she steers clear of alcohol and overindulging of any kind. However, a stranger would judge her harshly if they heard her reporting her blood levels by simply stating "I'm high again."

My sister, Erin, has many talents. Honesty is among them. Precisely because of her candor, I periodically seek her input on life's issues. Erin and her family came home for a vacation not so long ago and stayed with Husband and me. One morning, she accompanied me and Zeus on a hike through the park trails. As we walked, I mentioned my thoughts about Simon and this commissioning side of life. She made an interesting comment. She saw a long time ago that Husband and I were commissioned into service. We did not volunteer to be childless, but that status allowed us to be a couple with the time, finances, health, desire, and freedom to help when the need was clear. When all is said and done, being commissioned is a blessing for everyone involved. I'm sure Simon of Cyrene came to that same conclusion.

EYE-OPENER #7: *Doing God's will is a daily opportunity.*

Life's choices are not always black and white, right or wrong. I went through a stage of having trouble making decisions because I didn't know exactly what the Lord wanted for my life. Even though I had a strong desire to do His bidding, I was concerned about a long-term plan. It was bothersome that I couldn't grasp the bigger picture in figuring out where I was being led. A friend suggested talking to God about any uncertainty, tell Him what I think He's prompting me to do, and then go ahead with the plan of action. God is pleased with sincere aspirations. Based on my willingness to go where He leads, if I would get off track, I trust He won't let me get far before guiding me back to His blueprint.

It helped to reflect on the question, *How does one go about being proactive in following God's will?* Mary and Joseph did a rather good job of it, so it seemed appropriate to ponder what appeared to be their blueprint for following His will:

- They kept in touch with God through prayer, including listening and obeying.
- They obeyed the established religious laws of their time.

- They utilized God's gifts: His Spirit, faith, grace, and other people.

For example, the holy couple had Jesus circumcised eight days after birth in accordance with God's covenant law with Abraham (Luke 2:21). They also presented Jesus to God in the Jerusalem temple in accordance with the covenant law made with Moses. A holy man named Simeon was guided by the Spirit to go to the temple the same day the Holy Family entered. Prompted by the Spirit, he informed Mary and Joseph that their Baby was the awaited Messiah. Simeon declared to Mary that her Son would suffer, and she would suffer greatly as well (Luke 2:22-24). Though Mary may not have understood the full impact of Simeon's words, or to what events he was referring, she did not turn and run from an unknown future. Her faith told her that God would grant her the strength to proceed despite whatever trials came about. She prayed and pondered her way through it all, and she possessed a deep trust in the grace of God to carry her forward.

I also reflected on following God's will after hearing a particular sermon by a priest at Mass. His advice was to take one day at a time because each day is an opportunity to answer His call. His plan was:

- Take the time to pray, and tell God you are ready to do what He asks.

- Take the time to listen.

- The day will unfold, and God will present plenty of opportunity to take action.

That homily about daily opportunities brought to mind an experience I had in the grocery store. I was minding my own business pushing a cart through the aisles. There was another woman in the aisle who looked to be in her sixties. She appeared unkempt in clothes that were worn and mismatched. "Homeless" came to mind. The label seemed appropriate as I caught the stench of an unbathed body near the cans of tomatoes I leaned over. My nose automatically quit breathing in order to filter out the unpleasant odor. The tomatoes could wait. I piloted my cart around the corner to the shelves of cereal where the air would be fresher. Whew. *Thank God she didn't talk to me.* Oops. I unintentionally brought God into the event. I apologized to Him for my rude behavior toward the woman in the canned section even though she was not aware of it. *OK, Lord. She is your child, too. If you want me to start over, then bring it about. Help me do what I should do in Your name.* I realized I acted harshly in my heart. God had given me an opportunity to be Christ-like, and I blew it. The encounter did not require that I talk to her, but it did require that I not consider her less than me because she had less than me. I sincerely wanted a second chance to correct my attitude, but I was not going to pursue her. God knew I understood where I went wrong. If He wanted an interaction, the window would open itself without my forcing it. Further into the store, I turned down the soup aisle. She was there. Gentler inside than I had been previously, I was still minding my own business. She was approaching. Now she stood next to me. Her voice was clear and firm as she said, "Excuse me. Can you please tell me if these are the same thing?" She showed me two different brands of chicken bouillon. Her face showed me an aged, kind, beautiful woman with big eyes and soft features. "I'm shopping for someone else. I don't want to get the wrong item, but this other one costs less." She was thrifty, too. I asked her if I could take a minute to read the labels. She said, "please" and handed me the two containers. I put my glasses on, read the opposing labels, and gave her my advice. She thanked me with a smile. I replied, "You're welcome" and returned to my cart. This time my nose hadn't noticed a thing. On the way to the coffee section, I smiled my thanks to God for the almost missed opportunity to love a neighbor.

EYE-OPENER #8: *By striving to do God's will daily, we cooperate in His will that all might have eternal life.*

God's will is evasive at times. It can be frustrating trying to figure it out. Sometimes we confuse everything that happens in life as God's will. We get a less ominous picture by breaking the subject down a bit:

• **The big picture of God's will for all humankind**

Jesus told us He came to do the Father's will, which is ultimately:

That all who see the Son and believe in Him may have eternal life, and I shall raise him on the last day. (JOHN 6:40)

• **The smaller picture for us as individuals**

Within Scripture we can sort out what the big picture has to do with us, and how we help fulfill God's overall plan. We cooperate by following what the Son taught and living His example. Jesus instructs us, as individuals making up the whole, how to be proactive in the Father's ultimate will that everyone may have eternal life:

Just then a lawyer stood up to test Jesus. "Teacher," he said, "what must I do to inherit eternal life?" He said to him, "What is written in the law? What do you read there?" He answered, "You shall love the Lord your God with all your heart, and with all your soul, and with all your strength, and with all your mind; and your neighbor as yourself." And He said to him, "You have given the right answer; do this, and you will live." (LUKE 10:25-28)

Also for individual guidance in doing God's will, St. Paul, who became an apostle after Christ's death, put it very simply in his letter to the Thessalonians:

Rejoice always, pray without ceasing, give thanks in all circumstances; for this is the will of God in Christ Jesus for you.
(1 THESSALONIANS 5:16-18)

If we followed Jesus' instructions of loving God and neighbor along with St. Paul's advice to pray always, it would be difficult not to be drawn into thought, words, and deeds that cooperate in God's ultimate will that all may have eternal life. Constantly touching base with Him invites His response to shower down graces that guide us in our decision-making process. This important communication helps us fine-tune the ability to discern the presence of grace within daily routines as well as when weighing options for heftier endeavors. According to Christ, the choices we make each day should consider love for Him, our neighbors, and ourselves, and be void of detriment to anyone. Christ-like motivations in whatever we pursue are God's will for us as individuals. These motivations lead to accomplishing His will, in us and others, that all may have eternal life.

Unfortunately, life is full of uncooperative souls. Not everything people do and say is in accordance with God's will, but everyone still has the opportunity for eternal life because of Christ's death and resurrection. We have the choice to repent of wrongdoing and go forth in obedience. Disobedience is not God's will, but is of our own free will. It is not His will that a child be lost to drugs or alcohol, that a person abuse another, or that a plane be jettisoned into a tower to murder thousands of innocent victims. Poor choices have consequences that harm not only one's self, but others as well.

Knowing that no activity against God's will is able to thwart His plan of salvation through Christ, we find the ability to give thanks in all circumstances. In the midst of suffering, it may be difficult to verbalize thanksgiving, but our Lord knows the hearts of His children. He can read thanksgiving from afar as we cling to Him in silence when we cannot speak.

EYE-OPENER #9: *Our suffering can be offered to God in cooperation with His will that all may come to see, believe, and have eternal life.*

Looking back on those days of tirelessly, and then wearily, praying for a baby, I took a fresh look at Christ's life to teach me about suffering in disappointment. While praying to His Father in the garden of Gethsemane, Jesus poured His heart out. He asked God to have the cup of suffering pass Him by:

Then He withdrew from them about a stone's throw, knelt down, and prayed, "Father, if you are willing, remove this cup from me; yet, not my will but yours be done." (LUKE 22:41-42)

Christ did not get what He requested, but He got what He wanted. He wanted to cooperate with the Father's will that all may have eternal life. Thus He carried on and willingly entered into His passion. The suffering and death endured by Christ served to fulfill His Father's intentions for all of humanity. All of it for the greatest love one could offer, His life, so that we may have eternal life.

We, too, for love's sake, can "repurpose" our sufferings. As St. Paul tells us in Scripture:

I am now rejoicing in my sufferings for your sake, and in my flesh I am completing what is lacking in Christ's afflictions for the sake of his body, that is, the church. (COLOSSIANS 1:24)

Our own afflictions – big or small – are used in accordance with the Father's will when we offer them in prayer to Him for the sake of others. It is possible to endure our pains, disappointments, and bad times with joy knowing that God will take these hurts and use them for the good. Our sufferings, willingly joined in the image of Christ, become acts of love for souls in need of His grace, which, in turn, serve to build up individuals for the sake of the whole Body of Christ.

Frustration sets in when prayers have been offered asking to take the waiting, difficulty, or torment of a situation away, but the cup remains bitter. We must use Christ's example to trust the Father enough that we can drink what is set before us. Trust that God has heard your prayer, has taken it seriously, and is working with you – even if you cannot detect any activity. With the prayer "Thy will be done" in our hearts, every bit of suffering, of pain, of loss, of joy, of peace, of love, and of thanksgiving of every moment can be offered in accordance with His will. Then He shall raise us on the last day.

EYE-OPENER #10: *In sincerely wanting to do God's will, we seek His help.*

What we do on a daily basis can either coincide with God's plan for eternal life, or we can ignore His gifts, teachings, and expectations, and go about our business without Him. By asking for His help to walk through each day with Him as the lead, we surrender ourselves and our decisions in line with His will. In doing so, we trust that Father knows best and all will work out for the good.

God's will is for our sake, not His. He provides everything necessary to oblige in it if we choose. He gave us the Trinity: The

Father, Son, and Holy Spirit. Even God the Son became a living, human paradigm of going to God the Father in prayer and allowing the Spirit to move Him. Living as a human in all things except sin, Christ did not go about life without divine interaction with His Father. He showed by example how to be strong enough to do the Father's will. Jesus showed us not to go it alone.

Prior to going off to begin his public ministry to proclaim the Gospel, Jesus was baptized. As John the Baptist finished baptizing Him, the voice of the Father proclaimed Christ as His beloved Son, and the Holy Spirit descended upon Him (Matthew 3:13-17). Influenced by the Spirit, Jesus went off into the desert for 40 days to be with the Father in prayer and fasting. As His retreat ended, and He was spiritually full, He encountered and withstood the Devil's temptations to sin against His Father. After Satan departed, God sent angels to minister to His Son. (Matthew 4:1-11)

We, too, are called to prepare ourselves with the Spirit because we will be confronted with enticements that are not in our best interest, but they are alluring just the same. God does not leave us to fend for ourselves in a world full of temptation and suffering that might pull us away from Him. On the contrary, He provides the grace to face whatever unfolds. Every day offers the chance to proclaim one's self as God's child, to accept the gifts of the Spirit, to let Him accompany us into the desert, and to follow his direction. It is a direction that is not always on easy street. I found it interesting that God sent angels to minister to Jesus *after* He had the face-off with Satan in the desert. Sometimes we don't realize His peace until the worst is over, but we are tended to none-the-less.

In a restaurant a couple years ago, I had a stimulating conversation with an acquaintance regarding God's will. During our discussion, he asked if I thought God's will could be changed. My opinion was no. My explanation included the definition of His ultimate will – that all may have eternal life. God's will was, is, and always will be the same because He, in His perfection, never changes. Everything that happens on Earth is permitted by the Almighty without altering His ultimate plan. My friend disagreed with me because he believes prayer changes things – it can change the will of God. I agree prayer can indeed change things from our perspective, and sometimes in miraculous proportions. God is very much part of our lives because He wants us to succeed in fulfilling His will for ourselves and others to join Him eternally. The caveat is that God already expects us to change. He expects us to change things about ourselves that do not promote His will. Waiting for our readiness, He stands eager to shower us with graces to prompt change in line with His knowledge of our best interests. Those graces may change hearts, minds, situations, or heal bodies. For example, a person diagnosed with terminal cancer might become cancer free, leaving doctors baffled, because of the healing hand of the Almighty. In His divinity, He already knew healing would take place. However, that doesn't mean God's will was changed. Situations may change. We change. God's grace sometimes appears in miraculous ways as answer to prayer. Miracles hopefully promote an increase in faith and move us to share the love of God, which may lead others to what has always been God's will - that all may have eternal life.

God encourages us to communicate to Him what we want and need in this world, including the grace to change spiritually for the good. Sometimes we don't seek our Father's help until we are desperate. He patiently waits for us to engage Him, but that doesn't mean He is inactive toward us while He waits. He doesn't want to lose one person, so God will endlessly provide graces to stir a response. The tone of life, and many times the direction, is altered when we reach to accept those graces. He responds to our gestures toward Him. There are times when requests are granted and times when they are not answered with our desired outcome. In either case, needs are met according to God's wisdom.

I'm inclined to think that God acts and answers to invoke a positive, spiritual response on our parts. Notably answered prayers will likely move us into a more zealous relationship with our Father. It is then *our* wills that are changed through a fervent love for God. In turn, we transform our actions to become more Christ-like. Our Christ-like actions produce a domino effect by sparking better attitudes in those we've touched, and better attitudes may motivate others to also imitate Christ.

God's help is there. We only need to respond to it. His helping hand, full of grace, is at work to motivate the world to fall in line with His will that all may have eternal life.

GOD EXPECTS ME TO TRUST THAT HE IS ALWAYS THERE

Those who fear the Lord will not be timid, or play the coward, for he is their hope. Happy is the soul that fears the Lord! To whom does he look? And who is his support? The eyes of the Lord are on those who love him, a mighty shield and strong support, a shelter from scorching wind and a shade from noonday sun, a guard against stumbling and a help against falling. He lifts up the soul and makes the eyes sparkle; He gives health and life and blessing. (SIRACH 34:16-20)

My faith assures me that God is near in good times and in bad, in sickness and in health, and for richer and poorer. He has my standing invitation. He accepts it. I trust He is there.

EYE-OPENER #1: *God is there for all of His children whether they believe it or not.*

Now and then, an observation would seep into my thoughts and subtly try to escort me into that grey area of doubt. I saw plenty of people living life large who didn't count on God to be there; yet, they appeared to be successful and achieving wonderful things apart from Him. This prompted the question, *Why does it matter if I invite God to assist me in all of my endeavors or not?* After plenty of pondering, the faith-based reasoning I gave myself was:

- God is the creator of all life. Everyone, whether acknowledging His hand in it or not, has greatness, goodness, and talents knit into them by Him. We are designed in the image of God with the goodness of Him in our hearts. As we go out and live our lives, we have the freedom to be people of "good will" and allow our gifts to bear good fruit or to let our fruit spoil.

- Individuals do not have to believe God exists in order for Him to be present. The human definition of success can be reported by believers and non-believers alike. His manifestation is constantly in our midst, but people are not always aware of Him. If a person doesn't acknowledge God, then it makes sense that they will not acknowledge the signs of Him among us, either. Believe it or not, no one is truly apart from Him.

- The Scripture describing Pontius Pilate's interrogation of Jesus after His arrest is profound in its message. Christ stood before Pilate to be judged as a criminal. As a successful prefect of Rome, Pilate had the power to determine the fate of his prisoner. The mob outside called for Jesus to be crucified, but he knew the Man committed no crime. Pilate questioned Christ:

"Where are you from?" But Jesus gave him no answer. Pilate therefore said to Him, "Do you refuse to speak to me? Do you not know that I have power to release you, and power to crucify you?" Jesus answered him, "You would have no power over me unless it had been given you from above." (JOHN 19:9-11)

We can be successful and powerful in our own eyes, and the eyes of others, with not so much as a glance in God's direction. These powers have been given to us from God above. So it is with everyone. We are free to move about the world studying, researching, achieving, discovering, exploring, inventing, leading, marrying, parenting, and more with or without believing that it is He who allows us to move.

EYE-OPENER #2:   *We don't have to feel God's presence to trust that He is there.*

Periodically, I still get "pins and needles" while talking to God or being among others in His midst. Those hugs are a gift, but I don't routinely expect them. If it were up to me, I would prefer to have them all the time. It would be so nice to verify through this physical sign that God is with me every step I take. Whether it's forward or backward, He's there. Yes, it would be so nice, but faith requires an understanding that God does not continually give miraculous signs. My experience is that while I was a thirty-something-year-old baby of God trying to walk and stumble toward my Father, He encouraged me with a periodic hug as a sign of His presence.

It makes me a little sad to think that I needed "signs" back then to acknowledge God was there by my side. I consider my younger self a tad like the Apostle Thomas who wanted physical proof before He would believe Jesus rose from the dead. Christ granted Thomas the gift of proof, but Jesus also got the point across that true faith requires no proof:

> *But Thomas (who was called the Twin), one of the twelve, was not with them when Jesus came. So the other disciples told him, "We have seen the Lord." But he said to them, "Unless I see the mark of the nails in his hands, and put my finger in the mark of the nails and my hand in his side, I will not believe." A week later his disciples were again in the house, and Thomas was with them. Although the doors were shut, Jesus came and stood among them and said, "Peace be with you." Then he said to Thomas, "Put your finger here and see my hands. Reach out your hand and put it in my side. Do not doubt but believe." Thomas answered him, "My Lord*

and my God!" Jesus said to him, "Have you believed because you have seen me? Blessed are those who have not seen and yet have come to believe." (JOHN 20:24-29)

As I matured in faith, the physical sensations have grown fewer and further between. I trust He is there even without a corporal sign. This is faith.

It's important to note that physical signs, or "prayer fuzzies" as a fellow parishioner calls them, are not at all necessary in a relationship with God. Some are granted these gifts as encouragement even though they never doubted for a second. Many don't have any physical signs at all while enjoying a relationship with God. He shares His presence in different manners with different people for reasons known only to Him. Often it is the heart and soul of a person that "feels" the unique peacefulness of God's presence. Just as often very saintly people have no "feeling" that God is beside them, but in trust and faith they know He is there.

EYE-OPENER #3:   *It is in the difficulties of life that we can better understand the peace of God's nearness, which surpasses all understanding.*

The Lord is near. Do not worry about anything, but in everything by prayer and supplication with thanksgiving let your requests be made known to God. And the peace of God, which surpasses all understanding, will guard your hearts and your minds in Christ Jesus. (PHILIPPIANS 4:5-7)

Watching my father dramatically age over several years, I dreaded the day when my family would lose him. The day came in 2007. Dad's cancer was not caught until it was already in the fourth and final stage. Certainly, though, he had the disease growing in him for some time. Tests had been taken sporadically over the two years before diagnosis because Dad had a constant, nagging pain in his side. The results showed nothing. He endured life with his "imaginary" pain. Eventually, we were told by the doctors that pancreatic cancer is difficult to diagnose until the latter stage.

It was only after the diagnosis that I could see that God was there getting us ready months in advance. Hindsight has me convinced that an experience I had while on a retreat was the beginning of intercession from Heaven to prepare my family to handle the upcoming events.

The retreat was held toward the end of March 2007 at a convent situated on a large, serene piece of land. The weekend was hosted by a religious order of sisters and was attended by 23 women from my parish. Quite a bit of free time was planned in order to seek peace and quiet with God, but our group gathered several times a day to pray, share conversation, and enjoy meals. In between gatherings, each individual was able to use her free time in a manner that suited her needs and relationship with God. The retreat began Friday evening as we met in a community room where seating was arranged in a circle. Sister Kathleen was introduced to lead the group. Sister was in her seventies and quite stately. She asked us to go around the room, introduce ourselves, and give a tidbit about our name. My turn came up:

Hi. I was named after my Irish grandmother and great grandmother. I have two nicknames. One is "Mare" and the other is my Mom's nickname for me, "Mayme." That was my Irish grandmother's nickname, too. If I was a good kid, Mom used to send me off to bed with "Goodnight, Mayme." If I was not so endearing, she'd quip "Night, Mare!"

It wasn't until years later that I understood why Mom always wore a sly little grin all the while knowing that her reference to a nightmare was lost on me.

Saturday morning we joined in our circle after breakfast. Sister Kathleen explained that we would be using a form of prayer called "imagery." *Oh, no, please don't make me do this.* On the few occasions when I tried to meditate through imagery, my mind locked up. I'm supposed to clear my thoughts, but instead I become worried about silencing my brain. Sister continued, "Close your eyes and relax. Now, breathe deep," she said. "Breathe in and breathe out, breathe in and breathe out. Place yourself in the desert where it's peaceful. Yes, the desert can be peaceful. The sand blocks out the noise. There are no distractions. Place yourself in the desert." *OK, God. If I keep my eyes open, Sister will know I'm not going along. I'm going to close my eyes and try to use imagery. If You want me to do this for real, please help.* The next thing I know, I envision myself trudging in the desert. Then Jesus appears in front of me plodding in the same way. He's leading me through the sand making it easier for me. Jesus looked like the Jesus from the traditional pictures from my childhood. I only saw Him from the back, but recognized his wavy, brown hair and the long white robe with a red sash. Sister Kathleen says, "Now invite Jesus into your space in the desert." I'm thinking, *He's already here.* In a very rapid succession, the scene in my head changed. The exact same Jesus was also behind me. Then I saw an aerial view with Jesus as quadruplets surrounding me on all sides. Then it was gone.

Afterward, some of us shared our experience from the meditation. As I finished sharing, Evy asked if perhaps my Irish grandmother Mayme might have been helping me through the imagery. (My Irish Grandma passed away in the early sixties.) Then Lorraine informed us that Jesus on all four sides was part of an Irish blessing within St. Patrick's Breastplate. She e-mailed me the full prayer a few days later. A portion of it reads, "Christ with me, Christ before me, Christ behind me, Christ in me, Christ beneath me, Christ above me, Christ on my right, Christ on my left, Christ when I sit, Christ when I lie down, Christ when I arise."

After the Saturday morning session, we had a couple of hours to ourselves. Sister Kathleen suggested taking a stroll outside to meditate on the Stations of the Cross. The property included life-size statues depicting the agonizing walk of Christ as he was led along to be crucified. The 14 stations were spaced out over a mile's walk. It was decent enough weather to take the walk, pray, and meditate at each station. Sister recommended focusing our reflection on the hands of the different statues. At the first station we would notice Pilate washing his hands as he put the Lord's fate in the hands of the crowd. Along the way we would see a scene where Jesus meets his mother, and her hands are reaching out to her Son. At the station where Christ falls while carrying the cross, His hands are braced toward the ground to accept the fall. Sister directed us, "Look at the hands of the soldiers. Can you see angry hands? Are your own hands angry, or compassionate, or thankful?" The theme was hands and what they depict.

Sunday came. We met before dismissal to pray and share prior to the closing Mass. Sister Sarah took the lead for our circle and asked each woman to pair up with someone for the next segment. She explained that she would read aloud a prayer. As she did so, we were instructed to bless our prayer partner with the sign of the cross over each other's forehead, eyes, ears, mouth, hands, and feet. The gestures were in union with prayer that we may serve God and others. While waiting for Sister Sarah to begin, my eyes were lowered and fixed on my own hands resting on my knees. During the interim, my prayer partner, Sister Kathleen, put her hand on top of mine. I gasped. It was not her hand that I saw. The hand that flashed before me was that of my other grandmother, my Dad's mom who died in 1988. Her hands were always kind and nurturing. I didn't have time to react further because Sister Sarah was instructing us to turn to our partner and make the sign of the cross on her forehead. I turned to Sister Kathleen to sign. My eyes only caught her smile, but it was not hers. It was the unmistakable smile of my paternal Grandma.

The communion of saints became extremely personal that weekend. Both my grandmothers were spiritually with me through an amazing grace. They were already interceding as my father readied for death. From their home in everlasting life they were reaching out in prayer.

Two weeks after the retreat, Dad had a routine physical at which he confessed he still had his imaginary pain. The doctor examined Dad as usual, but this time he felt a lump. An MRI was scheduled for Dad's belly the following Friday. My parents received a call on Saturday from the doctor's office asking them to come in Monday to talk about the results. At this point, we were hoping the lump was an indication of another hernia because Dad had several over his adult life.

The day before Dad's appointment was Divine Mercy Sunday, and I was scheduled to participate in a parish seminar entitled "End of Life Issues." The main speaker was a nun, who was also a lawyer specializing in end of life legal matters. She was scheduled to talk for one hour on both the legalities and moral teachings regarding these emotional concerns.

Jerry was the second speaker. He was a cradle Catholic who drifted away from the Church. While faced with his mother's death, he had a conversion that brought him full force back to his Catholic faith. He began volunteering at a hospice after witnessing his mother's illness and dying moments. Jerry developed a devotion to Saint Faustina and the Divine Mercy prayers and promises. He was drawn to the saint's diary outlining her visions regarding God's Divine Mercy, which is Jesus. Her vision was of the risen Christ with two rays of light streaming from His heart, which depict the blood and water that gushed from His pierced side as He hung on the cross. One ray is white and represents our rebirth in baptism. The other is red and signifies Christ's sacrifice of body and blood, our redemption. During Jerry's presentation, he explained some of the promises Christ gave in association with His Divine Mercy message. One relates to praying the Divine Mercy prayer in the presence of the dying. Jesus promises to stand between His Father and the dying person, not as the Just Judge, but as the Merciful Savior.

Joe was the third guest. He shared his experience and blessing of being able to usher his wife into eternal life as she lost her battle with cancer. He shared with us a spiritual moment he had after his wife died. Joe's daughter and brand new granddaughter were staying with him over the days leading up to the funeral. At one point, His daughter was changing the baby in the bedroom, and he walked into the room to say something. As he crossed the threshold, he heard in his mind, "Baptize the baby at the funeral." Joe is adamant that it was his wife interceding and telling him what to do. He never would have thought to have a baptism and funeral on the same day, but that's exactly what Joe's family did. They celebrated both the baptism of the baby into her new, Christian life and the passing of his wife into her new, everlasting life.

Sister's presentation educated me on the legal matters involving death. There were documents for preparing a last will and testament and for preparing a living will. She spoke about the moral teachings the Church holds regarding a living will, and she explained the distinction between using ordinary and extraordinary means to keep a person alive. Before the evening was over, it also became clear that the Church made no distinction between "withholding" or "withdrawing" life supports when the decision to withdraw is based on failure of treatment to improve a person's health, and medical opinion no longer holds hope of it doing so. I took lots of notes because my parents were elderly, and the information may prove useful down the road.

The next day brought with it a new perspective. Dad was now both elderly and dying. During his Monday morning appointment, the doctor informed us that the MRI showed a growth on the pancreas. There was also a mass on the stomach. More tests were needed to confirm that he had pancreatic cancer, but that's what the doctor was inferring. Dad was admitted to the hospital, and the admissions packet included a copy of a living will. I read it. Had I not attended Sister's talk the previous day, seeing a living will in the packet would have been unfamiliar and upsetting. On the contrary, I was prepared.

Fresh in my mind was Jerry's talk on Divine Mercy Sunday about Christ's promises to St. Faustina. I researched the prayer devotion on the Internet. I began saying the Divine Mercy chaplet asking God to see my family through this difficult stretch of time with His peace and mercy. In the meantime, I had conversations with various people who also discovered the devotions. Rebecca began praying the Divine Mercy novena for the first time during that Easter season. My Aunt Leeny adopted the chaplet earlier that year. My Godson, Ryan, was attending a Catholic high school at the time and had just turned in an assignment about Divine Mercy. He mailed me a copy after hearing from his mom about my father's illness and my interest in this devotion. All this spiritual harmony, on top of the talk at the seminar, inspired me to ask other family members to adopt the prayers in unity asking God to see us through the coming storm. The chaplet became part of each day.

The family focus became Dad. Doctor appointments, chemotherapy, and oncology visits were family outings. Siblings living out of state flew home to see Dad for the last time. Life became a whirlwind, but somehow there was peace. Dad was being prepared for the promised everlasting life. There is peace in that.

Dad was serene for the most part. He didn't get angry, he didn't cry, he didn't argue. He accepted the verdict and chose chemotherapy. When Dad, Mom, and four of us sisters left the doctor's office, Dad suggested we go out to eat. I thought he must be in denial, or he didn't quite get the severity of the diagnosis. I was wrong. His reaction after that first big meeting with the oncologist seemed odd, but it was a noble reaction. Going out to eat after church was a tradition for my parents in their later years. We always knew where Mom and Dad would be after Sunday Mass. One, or two, or carloads of us would drop in on them and sit down to brunch. It often became a pleasant, but crowded, event instead of a romantic brunch for two. Dad wanted the comfort of that meal after he received the official diagnosis. So, we stopped to eat, made a toast to Dad with our coffee cups, and we were family.

My brother, John, flew home after hearing the verdict, and he stayed with my parents at their apartment. While he was there, our father had severe pain due to an obstruction and was rushed to the hospital by ambulance. I picked up John, and we drove to meet up with our folks. By the time my brother and I arrived at the hospital, the emergency was over. Dad was able to go home, but first he wanted the four of us to stop for lunch. We accommodated his request without hesitation. Dad had lost all but the slightest sense of taste and had no appetite. He could no longer enjoy food. The request to eat out was not for him, but it was a familiar way to spend precious time with those he loved. I can't help but be reminded that Christ's invitation to eat the Eucharistic meal at each Mass is not for His sake, but for those he loves.

Leading up to Dad's passing, we were given the gift of two months. Two months to not take him for granted. Two months to love him to death. He could not do much for himself anymore. Mom did it for him. My parents shared an apartment in a retirement community. They lived there together until Dad was transferred to the on-campus nursing facility five days before he died. I watched my mother love my father for better and for worse in their apartment until it became absolutely necessary for hospice care. As I grow old with Husband, God grant me the kind of love Mom had for Dad that she could clean up one accident after another when Dad couldn't quite make it to the bathroom. God grant Husband and me that kind of love so we can love each other unto the moment of death in whatever form it takes.

Throughout Dad's illness, he graced us with his humor and strength so we could laugh through the tears. I'll remember forever the hearty laughter in the hospital room on one particular day when Husband and I went to see Dad. My father was uncomfortable because his body slid down low on the bed. He was too weak to push himself back up so Husband offered to help. The attractive nurse in the room instructed Husband to lean over Dad's other shoulder, grab the sheet-pad under his upper torso, and help pull him up. On her cue, they resituated the ailing man on his bed. Husband hovered over Dad waiting for a signal that his duty was done. As he lingered, his face was oh-so-close to my father's. Dad opened his mouth to speak. We waited for something profound. As the words slowly made their way to the surface we heard, "Boy, are you ugly!" Comparing his son-in-law to the pretty nurse became the last sentiment my Dad uttered to my spouse. Anyone unfamiliar with the relationship and humor shared between the two might think those to be harsh words. To Husband, they were spoken with love.

Each of Dad's children came home from whatever distance hoping to spend time with him while he was still aware. God gave us so many blessings through the worst of everything. Our father was showered with grace by three holy sacraments received as he lay in bed waiting: Reconciliation, the Eucharist, and Anointing of the Sick. Family members did plenty of praying at his bedside and, more than once, recited in trusting unison the Divine Mercy chaplet. Counting on the promise that Christ would greet Dad as the Merciful Savior, not as the Just Judge, I asked my father to let us know if Jesus kept his promise.

We took the time to talk, to pray, to dote on, and to shower attention and love on Dad. I wanted to give so much more as he lay there, but didn't know how to reveal it. My heart was gushing with emotion, but I couldn't physically or verbally rid myself of it. It became spiritual love because nothing else was needed on this Earth for my Dad. The closer he came to being privy to the promises of our faith, the purer love became. There was no time to be petty, impatient, or regretful about the things we did, or failed to do, that irritated one another. The past no longer existed. There were no distractions or interferences to taint the love being poured out by all. There was only the present moment, which was blossoming with God's love and grace.

The time was short, but merciful. Dad did everything quickly. He jumped from one stage of dying into another without commotion and didn't stay long before moving on to the next. Despite the swiftness, waiting and watching for the death of a beloved most certainly is painful suffering. We shared his anguish. In the depths of hurt, comfort exists knowing that Christ went through human suffering for the sake of The Truth. Striving to be Christ-like creatures living His Truth, we must expect no less. Reaching its crescendo, Dad's suffering was coming to an end. Barely able to respond as his body was shutting down, I leaned against my father's face and asked him to picture himself against the foot of the cross as Christ hung upon it. Merge the agony with His, Daddy, and give it all to Jesus. There is comfort there.

Family members took turns holding vigil by Dad's bedside. When the shift changed, at least one remained while the others curled up on the couch or chair in a nearby "family room." Rebecca had gone home to rest after her vigil the night before. Hannah took Mom back to the apartment to try for some much needed sleep. My sisters, Josie and Emily, went back to the waiting room to catch a breather. It was my turn to stay. If anything changed, I would call. Dad was unresponsive, but I was hopeful he could hear. I prayed. I talked. I told him so much that never needed to be said before. Since it was just the two of us, I was quite honest. I gave him a to-do list with enough on it to keep him busy during eternal life. Beginning with Mom, I named my way through the oldest child to his youngest, his grandchildren, and then his great granddaughter. I asked Dad to talk to Jesus about each of our unique needs. Time was passing. Without thinking, I was counting the seconds between Dad's breaths. When the seconds jumped from two to four, I ran to the waiting room to get Emily and Josie. It was time to usher this dying man into his new and everlasting home. We called Mom and Hannah on the cell phone and told them to come quickly. Surrounding him once again, Emily, Josie, and I began saying the Divine Mercy Chaplet. As we neared the end of the chaplet, Dad took one long breath. Then we heard the silence of nothing. "DAD!" He took another long breath and finally one more.

Hannah and Mom entered the room moments later. Mom was upset that she wasn't there, but we think her spouse wanted to spare her that most difficult goodbye. He quietly left without a fuss. Recounting the moments at home, I walked Husband through everything. He perceived Dad's three last breaths as a goodbye to each of us hovering over him, one for Josie; one for Emily; one for me.

The two months leading to Dad's death had my family entangled in suffering topped with God's pure love, compassion, mercy, grace, peace, and joy. Compare suffering to a baked potato. How many people choose to eat a baked potato with nothing on it? It's like forcing yourself to eat the thing dry just because it's good for you. Put too much of a dry potato in your mouth, and it feels like you have to choke it down. It's a whole different approach if you top that potato with butter, chili, onion, crispy bacon, cheese, and sour cream. The toppings bring joy to the meal and a whole new attitude toward the experience. That's the same with suffering. Suffering in itself can choke a person into darkness. If you choose to smother the suffering with unceasing prayer and God's buffet of graces, then the light of Christ's presence breaks through the darkness and replaces it with peace and understanding. My family included God in every step during Dad's illness and subsequent death. It's what faith requires. It's how our faith preserves us from choking. We loaded the suffering with God's promise that in death we find life as He always meant it to be.

God fed us a spiritually loaded baked potato during those months of upheaval and grief. He gave Dad all the toppings, and He shared them with our family. There was enough for everyone. No matter where our hearts were spiritually, all were fed. God prepared us. He was merciful. There was peace amidst pain. God was there.

EYE-OPENER #4: *It's not a coincidence. It's God. He is there.*

Author SQuire Rushnell wrote the book "When God Winks,"[7] which introduced me to the notion that God "winks" at us in what

---

7 SQuire Rushnell, *When God Winks*, (Atria Books: New York 2001)

we might call a coincidence. His book brought to mind the many times I have heard people say, "There are no coincidences." Instead, God blesses us in our daily lives through people, creatures, places, events, and things that cross our paths. I firmly believe He uses circumstances to get a message across to a person in need of hearing. I believe, and yet, there are times when I must remind myself to stand back and view the picture to find God's fingerprints all over the scene.

After a trip to Italy, I am able to recollect a few "coincidences" that I prefer to think of as a wink from God.

One such experience begins at a Mass in the winter of 2004 when an announcement was made regarding an 11-day pilgrimage to Italy scheduled for the fall of 2005. Within 10 seconds of hearing the invitation, I processed the information, thought I would love to go, dismissed such a trip because of costs involved, and let my mind move on to the next announcement. On the way out the door after Mass, Husband grabbed a flyer detailing the trip. He wanted me to go because he knew my heart. This was a gift accepted with much gratitude.

There were many incidents in Italy that brought out different emotions, tugged at my senses, and tested my energy levels. The majority of encounters were down to earth, and my reactions to these events were of the human nature sort. This was disappointing because I had conjured up an idea of the trip being full of heavenly, miraculous happenings. After all, it was a spiritual pilgrimage. The reality of it is that we live life as humans. Our experiences are seen and felt through humanness. There were times on the pilgrimage when I had trouble detecting a holy, spiritual joy because I was distracted by the crowded presence and business of other people. That's life. Even so, there were moments when I was positive God was winking, but I couldn't snap His picture to prove it.

I was truly excited about the visit to St. Peter's Square for the weekly, public audience with the Pope. John Paul II passed away in April of 2005. Pope Benedict XVI became his successor. Several from our tour group of 40 woke up at 5:00 a.m. to head to the Square for the scheduled Wednesday audience. Their intent was to get in line early enough to find seats close to where the Popemobile would make its rounds. They hoped to reserve space for those of us arriving later on the tour bus. Our bus arrived two hours before the scheduled activities. We walked from the drop-off point to the Square, and our sights were set on finding the early risers. The search started as we entered at the back of the sea of chairs arranged for the anticipated crowd. The rear seats were empty, but the front section closest to the podium was filling up fast. It was difficult for all of us to stick together as we got into the thick of the audience. Some of my comrades opted to take the first available seat rather than go forward. I pressed on. It was difficult to see over all of the heads as I waded through the aisles searching for familiar faces. My name was being called by a female voice in an attempt to lead me to my associates, but I couldn't see a face to go with it. I moved through the crowd in the direction I was being called. Meanwhile, the tour guide accompanying our group was at my side. She was not happy with my technique of advancing, which required excusing myself to squeeze over the knees of row upon row of seated people. It seemed to her that only Americans behaved as if they were at a football game. Her admonishment made me feel guilty for several minutes, but I saw no other way to find the friendly voice on the other side. Pressing on without her, no one else seemed to mind my determination. Instead, they egged me on to the voice. My guess was that most of those seated were foreigners, too. I had my own fan club of strangers helping me to my destination. While considering giving up to take a seat in the empty area behind me, I heard an unfamiliar, male voice calling my name. The sound was closer than the voice coming from the original direction. He shouted my name several times until my eyes came in contact with the voice's owner. He was smiling and waving me on. "Over here. There's a seat reserved just for you." My plans changed at this alternative news. Within a minute, I was seated next to this stranger. He was a monk named Gino from Texas sitting amongst his own tour group. I now occupied the one empty chair in his section. It was in the second row! I sat down and enjoyed my own little miracle. When Pope Benedict XVI finally made his rounds in the Popemobile, I snapped his picture. His smiling face now hangs on the wall with the family photos at home.

Friday before leaving Rome to go home, the group had a free day with no scheduled activities. A few of us chose to go to the tomb of Pope John Paul II. Upon entering the tunnel leading to his resting place underneath St. Peter's Basilica, I was greeted with that tingling sensation of a hug. It seemed God was hovering over us as we approached the Pope's grave. We arrived early enough so there was not yet a line forming in the corridor. The first memorial was his. The lack of a crowd allowed us to pause in silence uninterrupted for some time before moving on to the Apostle Peter's burial site. There was a guard stationed at the Pope's tomb to ensure that no one hopped over the rope barrier. He was within arm's reach. I whispered a request, handed him a medal purchased for my mother-in-law, and gave him a scrap of paper, which listed the names of people I prayed for in every church I entered in Italy. When I asked him to touch these two items to John Paul II's unassuming marker, he did so without hesitation. I thanked him kindly. Minutes later a swarm of people walked down the entrance toward the tomb. Similar requests were made from various visitors, but the guard would not accommodate them. I believe the size of the group kept him from honoring additional favors to avoid disrupting the quiet atmosphere and distracting him from his sentinel duties. I silently thanked God for the guard's kindness.

A couple years after the trip to Italy, there was another occasion when I found myself thinking, *What a coincidence.* I got up that Wednesday morning before the sun and I was wide awake. Sipping my coffee, I just knew that I would accomplish everything on my list that day. My schedule included going to noon Mass. As I was getting cleaned up to go to church, my thoughts turned to sadness over so much in the world that was wrong. The world continues to push God further away. I considered not going to Mass. *Help, Lord. Please. The state of the world is depressing. I don't like this blue mood that keeps me from You.* Even while telling God about the state of things, I continued my get-ready-to-go-out routine, got in my car, and began to drive. So saddened by thought, it crossed my mind to run errands instead, or maybe I would just go home. In prayer, I asked God to help me get to Mass so I could make a perfect offering for the world's woes. I would offer back the gift of His dearly beloved Lamb within the Eucharist. I pulled into the church lot and attended Mass.

During the priest's homily, I sat back and listened. Father announced that it was the feast day of Blessed Mother Theresa of Calcutta. I didn't know that. He continued with a summary of her story. She's the famous nun that served the poor, dying people in the streets of Calcutta, India. She died in September of 1997. A decade later, her spiritual director decided Mother Theresa's journals should be released to the public. The journals reveal that she suffered from "the dark night of the soul." The secular world would refer to this as depression and might suggest she obtain antidepressants from her doctor. Father went on to explain that this condition of the soul is spiritual. Yes, there is medically diagnosed depression in our world, but this was spiritual for Mother Theresa. Her burden of feeling so isolated from God did not turn her away from her daily mission to serve the poor of Calcutta. Instead, the torment within her soul joined her to Christ's suffering and bonded her to Him in a way most of us never experience.

My insides jumped upon hearing the word "depression" thrown back at me from the conversation with God earlier that morning. I got the message. There will be days when I don't feel spiritually connected and upbeat while trying to live life according to God. So be it. I must persevere in my relationship and remember the desire to hand myself over to Him on a daily basis. Feelings don't define His presence. Perseverance is key. Trust is vital. God is there.

God surprised me again on June 30, 2011, but I did not realize it while it was happening. It began on a Thursday morning while walking Zeus. I was praying the rosary and just beginning to con-template the mystery of the Wedding of Cana (John 2:1-11). At this wedding, the Blessed Mother went to bat for the families of the bride and groom because the wine ran out. She talked to Jesus on their behalf and explained the situation to Him. Her Son provided for their needs by transforming water into wine. Prior to starting the prayers for that mystery, I had asked Mary to intercede and take my intentions before Her Son. I gave her a whole list of needs for family and friends. I also asked my dearly departed Dad to pray with me. As I silently gave Mary the litany of names and requests, I remembered to add the relatives on my Dad's side living in the Carolinas. This was, sadly, unusual for me to include them in my prayers, not because I didn't care, but because I plain forget. Even more unusual, I included the name of my Dad's sister-in-law, my Aunt Mickey, who was 90 years old. She was the only name I said aloud, and I said it with an emotional urgency. Later that afternoon, Rebecca called to tell me that Aunt Mickey passed away earlier in the day. She proceeded to tell me that these Southern relatives had been on her mind the last couple weeks. That prompted her to search for our cousin Claudia on Facebook. The two were in touch, and Rebecca was informed that Aunt Mickey had been in the hospital for a short span before her death that morning. My brother, John, subsequently shared that this side of our family had recently been in his thoughts and prayers. Perhaps my Dad joined his prayers with ours, and signaled us to pray for our Aunt and her family in a time when they needed the peace of God.

God works, or perhaps He winks, in mysterious ways.

GOD EXPECTS ME TO DEVELOP VALUES THAT REFLECT HIS IMAGE

You were taught to put away your former way of life, your old self, corrupt and deluded by its lusts, and to be renewed in the spirit of your minds, and to clothe yourselves with the new self, created according to the likeness of God in true righteousness and holiness. (EPHESIANS 4:22-24)

So then, putting away falsehood, let all of us speak the truth to our neighbors, for we are members of one another. Be angry but do not sin; do not let the sun go down on your anger, and do not make room for the devil. Thieves must give up stealing; rather let them labor and work honestly with their own hands, so as to have something to share with the needy. Let no evil talk come out of your mouths, but only what is useful for building up, as there is need, so that your words may give grace to those who hear. Put away from you all bitterness and wrath and anger and wrangling and slander, together with all malice, and be kind to one another, tenderhearted, forgiving one another, as God in Christ has forgiven you. Therefore be imitators of God, as beloved children, and live in love, as Christ loved us and gave Himself up for us a fragrant offering and sacrifice to God. (EPHESIANS 4:25-29, 31-32 AND 5:1-2)

Some of us successfully live and work together in tandem and peace. Others live and work together with bitterness and turmoil. It is thought provoking to sit back and try to figure out why some individuals, families, employees, employers, church members, or community residents seem to function with more life and joy in their steps than others. Perhaps it is that the more members involved who follow the prescription of good will toward others, the more they promote a good, happy, peaceful environment for the organization as a whole. If the machine isn't running so smoothly or morale is low, the questions to be asked may be: Are ethics put forth that consider the good of others or is self-satisfaction the driving force? Do those involved reach out to others in need or turn a blind eye? Are the members forgiving or spiteful because they cannot forgive? Are they unselfish or greedy? Do they tell the truth or lie? Are they sober or drunk? Are they honest or cheaters? Are they prideful or humble? Adopting personal values that include being kind to others creates a ripple effect that boosts the morale and lives of those around us. Then, those around us may likely be motivated to live "*according to the likeness of God in true righteousness and holiness.*"

Over the decades, our society as a whole has been cultivated to live for the moment, seeking immediate gratification with goals that focus on self-preservation and material things. Along with this lifestyle comes a lack of responsibility and concern for any consequences affecting others. Self-centered freedom has laid a foundation for new norms in our culture, which brings with it chaos within families, within schools, within communities, within society, and worst of all, it sets the same stage for our future youth who won't know any better.

EYE-OPENER #1:   *God's code of ethics is not being handed down clearly or completely to the children of today.*

You shall put these words of mine in your heart and soul, and you shall bind them as a sign on your hand, and fix them as an emblem on your forehead. Teach them to your children, talking about them when you are at home and when you are away, when you lie down and when you rise. (DEUTERONOMY 11:18-19)

And, fathers, do not provoke your children to anger, but bring them up in the discipline and instruction of the Lord. (EPHESIANS 6:4)

Back in my younger adult days, I received counsel from a psychologist who gave me advice strictly from a secular point of view. Freshly armed with this worldly picture, I ignored the religious residue in my conscience and continued my path down the ancient ruins. Today's children don't need to walk down the path. They are born smack-dab in the middle of the ruins. I see a generation of children in their teens and early 20s who are innocent in their destructive choices because they have been taught by example that what is wrong is right. The examples come from a generation or two of religious lukewarmness in modern parenting, and from educational and governmental systems increasingly devoid of God because someone may be offended at His mention. Simply put, our children of today don't know any better because they have not been taught that what God expects is for their own physical, emotional, and spiritual welfare.

Examples of philosophies, which if embraced rather than dismissed as old fashioned, may steer our children to a healthier state of being:

1. **Drugs, alcohol, and sex are not healthy pieces of childhood.**

The majority of the teenage boys housed at the Youth Development Center where I conducted the Bible study class barely knew God. They weren't taught about Him except for a mention here or there from a grandmother or an elder aunt in passing. Illegal gun and drug activity, gang violence, and prostitution were common family threads. The mindset among these young men was that serving jail time was a natural part of life. Some were already fathers, but few were married. Parenting from prison, therefore, seemed normal as well. These incarcerated young men talked freely about having a parent, sibling, or other close relative who also did jail time. Being locked up somehow became prestigious.

2. **The "sexual revolution" was/is self-centered mayhem.**

The definition of "a troubled teen" does not only apply to youth who get into trouble at school, dropout, or end up with arrest records. "Troubled" is a title that can be applied to just about every teen in mainstream America struggling with both peer pressure and society's commercialized encouragement to enter sexual adulthood earlier and earlier. Perhaps I shouldn't use the word "struggling" across the board because a large segment of our teens have no qualms about entering "sexhood" sooner than later. Society glamorizes uncommitted sex so much that adolescents are embarrassed to admit they are not having sex. Pregnancy has become trendy, but these child moms and dads make for ill-equipped and immature parents. Realistically, the responsibility of raising babies of teenagers defaults to grandparents, charitable organizations, and/or government funding. Thankfully, there are grandparents and assistance available to give these new families a fighting chance to thrive when the initial odds are against them.

My niece Mandy was a prime example of an average teenager's introduction to sexual activity. Unenthusiastic about her Christian faith, she was absorbed with the things that enthralled her peers. As sweet as she was, she was not perceptive of the sacrifices her parents made to provide a home for her and her siblings, Sherri and Don. She was typical. Her pregnancy was predictable. Her outlook on sex was a Hollywood glossed attitude that it's what girls and boys do. In her mind she was a grownup, her parents were old fashioned, and they had no clue of how mature she was as a high school junior. Mandy became pregnant at 16 years of age. Had it not been for the support of her parents, siblings, and reliance on government aid for single moms, she would have found herself on the street with no high school diploma, no money, and no job while raising her child alone. It was time to become a grownup for real.

Mandy shared a room with her sister before the baby was born. The grandparents-to-be converted their dining room into a bedroom offering privacy for mother and child. It also made it nice for Sherri who enjoyed the ability to sleep at night. Mandy was able to finish high school and attend college because family members took babysitting shifts so she could continue her education. It was a grown-up decision to want to finish school and get a college education. It was not so mature to ask relatives to continue babysitting duties into the evening, which allowed her to maintain the social life of a teenager.

As time and experience teach, this maturing young lady began to think and act like a responsible adult mom. Interest in her spiritual life also blossomed. My niece came to appreciate the opportunity her support group had given her to become self-sufficient instead of remaining a dependent child with a child. Mandy has since married a true love, and together they raise three wonderful children.

3. **Social Justice offers assistance to enable others to stand on their own.**

The term "social justice" is a popular topic in today's political arena. The definition of social justice in its truest sense must be based on the truth and light of Christ's teachings. It is structured to always consider the dignity of every individual served and strives for positive development of the person. Successful public programs are meant to lend a hand to those who are down, with the intent of lifting them up to become as independent as possible. They, in turn, strive to be charitable to others in accordance with their own gifts and talents.

Following Mandy's situation, it developed to portray the purpose of social justice perfectly. She accepted the help of family and government aid in order to survive the storm of uncertainty as an adolescent, single mom. She came to see the charity given to her as a gift. Such an attitude sparked her maturing heart to yearn to give charity freely to others. The wisdom gained through adversity developed into concern for others in similar circumstances. As Mandy reached her mid-twenties, she began to use her talents to help other single moms get on their feet. She reached out to families in a nearby homeless shelter because she understood how close anyone can come to living on the edge. She volunteered her services by organizing a tutoring program to help children in the shelter with academic basics. From experience, she knew how important education and encouragement were for these disadvantaged youngsters in order to move toward independence. She wanted to "give back" some of the support she was given when she needed it most.

More recently, Mandy oversaw the startup of a secondhand clothing boutique and managed operations after the store opened. The mission of this non-profit endeavor was to hire women receiving public assistance and help them achieve the goal of self-sufficiency. The organization provided these women work experience, business attire at a discounted price, and interview instruction in an effort to promote the confidence and skills necessary to enter the job market. The concept offered a good training ground and encouraged employees as they worked toward their goals. All proceeds went back into the program to hire future women in need.

Mandy's compassion continues to move her to give back from her own gifts and talents. The transformation of this young woman growing up in God has been beautiful to watch.

4. **Marriage is sacred before God.**

Then the Lord God said, "It is not good that the man should be alone; I will make him a helper as his partner." Therefore a man leaves his father and his mother and clings to his wife, and they become one flesh. (GENESIS 2:18, 24)

I've often thought about a conversation I had with a co-worker back in the early nineties. Brenda was a single mom taking college classes at night. She knew I had grown in my faith, and we had a conversation regarding a discussion that took place in her social studies class. The professor was theorizing that marriage is not biblical, but was made up by a primitive culture living in a time when social norms were restrictive and non-tolerant. Marriage was apparently invented as a way of controlling people, jealousy, and gossip. I disagreed, but at the time, I didn't know enough about Scripture to convey God's concepts on holy matrimony.

The number of young couples choosing to live together instead of getting married continues to climb. This rite of passage seems to be more of a testing ground versus an indicator of true, forever love. Example has our high school graduates running off to adulthood with a definition of love that does not include God. The message being absorbed by the young is that marriage doesn't matter. Au contraire, God expects us to remember that marriage is holy. Mainstream America has lost this notion. We the people have become lukewarm about the sacredness of the marriage covenant, and that attitude is reflected in our children. It is understandable (even to God, I'm sure) that those having a cold relationship with God would exclude inviting Him into a love relationship. What doesn't make sense is that more and more people of faith, those proclaiming that God is their God, are stopping short of taking vows before Him. It is this lack of desire by the faithful to invite Him to be the center and foundation of a relationship that does not compute. Having a strong, mature, living faith should culture a desire to run to Him to bless the relationships we keep. If a person of faith is not willing to go before Him with a beloved and enter into a marriage covenant, either the bond with God or the bond with the declared loved one is missing something. At the same time, we shouldn't run to the altar only to satisfy family tradition and expectations. Prior to entering into the marriage covenant before God, He should be consulted and invited into the relationship. It takes serious prayer and lots of it. Before, during, and after!

5. **Physical intimacy is a gift from God and is to be given and received in holiness.**

When God created man and woman, He made them in His image. Therefore, they were created in holiness and love. He blessed them as he joined the two to become one flesh, and then He told them to be fruitful and multiply:

> *So God created humankind in his image, in the image of God*
> *he created them; male and female he created them. God blessed*
> *them, and God said to them, "Be fruitful and multiply."*
> *(GENESIS 1:27-28)*

Forgive me, but the Genesis account of God blessing the first couple, sending them off to become one flesh, and to have children reminds me of the childhood rhyme often sung while jump roping:

> *First comes love, then comes marriage, then comes so-and-so in*
> *a baby carriage!*

It is enlightening to note that God gave the couple His blessing *before* instructing them to be fruitful and multiply. This is holy matrimony. Marriage was God's idea. He invented it. Within this bond, God blesses the couple with the physical gift of intimacy where the two become one flesh. Within this physical union, the couple becomes one flesh in a miraculous way when the two become one in the form of a child.

Blessed by God, not only is the marriage to be holy, but the physical union between husband and wife is to be holy. Through the grace of God, we are indeed capable of having sex the way He intended us to have it; that is, in holiness. To love in holiness is to give the gift of one's entire physical, mental, and emotional being to one's spouse. A couple gives themselves not only to each other, but in union they give themselves totally to God. Total giving does not include taking, but yields receiving. There is a universe of difference between taking and receiving. When both spouses give 100% of themselves without self-motivation, the giving becomes a gift back as well. There is no need to take.

Even though I had asked God to help me decide if Mister was the right guy, my view on marriage was marred by daily exposure to relationships stimulated by a secular world. What I saw over and over again was infidelity and lots of divorce. It was all so common and acceptable. If things didn't work out, divorce was a viable option. When I accepted Mister's proposal, we automatically planned a church wedding, but I didn't extend a sincere invitation to God to bless our union. He wasn't really in my circle of friends or relatives at the time. Fortunately, He was there, anyway. After all, the ceremony was held in His house!

Had I not eventually invited God back into my life and marriage, I believe Husband and I may have tinkered with divorce years ago because I didn't know how to be married and think as a unit. Instead God gave me an extreme, internal makeover that took me from a "me first" and "how will it affect me" attitude to looking at things from an "us" perspective. I had been on my own for over a decade prior to marriage. The "me, myself, and I" survival mode was deeply embedded. God used Husband as a visual aide to teach me "the two shall become one" concept of love.

Jesus is not ignorant of such things as human sexuality. He understands that our brain chemistry is programmed to react physically to stimuli that attract us. God created us in such a way that we long for our mate. Otherwise, we might not think it worth the labor pains to be fruitful and multiply. Human sexuality is a pleasurable, natural gift from our Creator. What is natural for humans, however, does not equate to what is natural for the beasts He created. Human physical intimacy is to be born of the purest love; not that of dogs and cats that satisfy urges anytime nature calls. Nature also calls for some animals to kill their young, but most of us think it morally innate for humans to use restraint when the itch develops to strangle a rebellious child. Thank Heaven we are wired so we do not react immediately upon every impulse. To some extent, even our society agrees that people are capable of controlling themselves because not doing so may lead to incarceration.

Healthy people do have control of their bodily functions. We control our bladders, our appetites, our tempers, and our voices. God gave us the ability to tame our sex drive as well, and lest we forget, He gave us the Holy Spirit to help us conquer temptations by utilizing self-control. He expects us to have discipline or to gain it by calling upon the Spirit for help in this matter:

> *For this is the will of God, your sanctification: that you abstain from fornication; that each one of you know how to control your own body in holiness and honor, not with lustful passion, like the Gentiles who do not know God; that no one wrong or exploit a brother or sister in this matter ... For God did not call us to impurity but in holiness. Therefore whoever rejects this rejects not human authority but God, who also gives His Holy Spirit to you. (1 THESSALONIANS 4:3-8)*

When Jesus saw the crowds, he went up the mountain; and after he sat down, his disciples came to him. Then he began to speak, and taught them, saying: … "You have heard that it was said, 'You shall not commit adultery.' But I say to you that everyone who looks at a woman with lust has already committed adultery with her in his heart." (MATTHEW 5:1, 27)

We have been tutored with societal notions and theories that we cannot control our sexual appetites. As each generation is spawned, sex becomes more commercialized with advertisers and the media as head cheerleaders. On a positive note, at least some of the TV talk shows, reality shows, and soap operas have unwittingly revealed the undesirable traits bred within the trend of casual sexual intimacy. These ugly traits include: jealousy, paranoia, mistrust, broken hearts, lack of confidence, lack of commitment, lack of responsibility, confusion, depression, anxiety, anger, stalking, violence, an upswing in the paternity test business, and abortions.

Sex has also become a readily accessible, computerized, performance-oriented spectator sport that has record numbers of young people (not to mention older adults) addicted to fantasies. This exploitation of "a brother or sister in this matter" leaves unrealistic expectations of what intimacy should be when our young ones finally find their "soul mate." Addictions damage relationships. With all of the "advances" in sex education, the holiness and loving commitment of it all is missing in the translation. Society promulgates lust, not love. Tina Turner's hit song, "What's Love Got to Do with It"[8] has become the scary norm. Love making is not promoted as the special, intimate, holy, forever bond that reflects a gift from God. Our children need to be deprogrammed from the cultural, generic definition of sexual intimacy which equates to a self-centered, uncontrollable, casual, dating game with no commitment necessary.

---

8 Terry Britten, Graham Lyle, "What's Love Got to Do with It?" (Recorded by Tina Turner) on Private Dancer Album (Los Angeles: Capitol Records 1984)

As if the casual take on God's gift of intimate love were not sad enough, the teens and young adults of today are becoming more delusional in their idea of healthy, intimate, physical relations. Perhaps it is the excess of pornography that has brought our youth to the point of no return where the thrill of one-on-one sex is no longer enough; and where unrealistic computer images burned into the mind's eye no longer satisfy. Perhaps in this glut, people are losing the ability to function in a healthy, sacred, monogamous relationship that God excpects of us. There is help to be had for those with sex addictions and obsessions. Unfortunately, the public at large is in denial that a huge problem exists, so our teens and young adults are not told to get help, and they don't realize they need it. Pornography advocates cling to the defenses of free speech and press, and then claim the right to distort minds and bodies without limit. A sugar coating is added by stating that exploiting men and women in this way does no harm. I vehemently argue with that viewpoint after being educated on effects of habitual X-rated medium used by teenagers. Most of the residents at the YDC prison were raised as children with free access to porn. The most shocking reality was of an inmate, who was only 13 years of age, convicted of raping his sister after viewing a pornographic movie.

Within this last year, I have cried over more than one headline report of teens who have sexually abused someone else, usually with excessive alcohol or drugs involved. The new twist gaining momentum is that juveniles are committing these crimes in public. Onlookers are numb to the evil that is happening. No one makes a move to call for help or stop the madness. Instead, cell phone videos are rolling to catch the "excitement," and a race ensues to get the action on "YouTube." If this is not the consequence of a Godless society, I don't know where we have to go to prove we are already there. As a society, we are failing to teach our children well.

Jesus taught holy love in every sense of the term whether it be of the physical or spiritual nature. Pure love is not self-centered. His definition of love is not meant to use people for one's own satisfaction. Nor is it genuine love to leave a trail of hurt or broken hearts while pursuing short-term affection. Yes, we may choose to sleep with anyone and everyone we please, but that does not make it the morally right thing to do. Yes, we can control ourselves, but instead we have learned to entertain our yearnings and hide God in the closet until finished.

It is not yet lust when the brain signals a physical attraction to another person. It becomes lust when a person allows the mind to take the signal, rev up the engine and turn another being into a sexual object to satisfy selfish intentions. The key to avoiding lust is using God's blueprint for sexual intimacy instead of the world's proposal. This means either taking the brain signal and using it in accord with the Creator's design for pure love or restraining the signal. Like anything else in life, if you have difficulty doing things His way, it's a good idea to ask Him to assist. Through the gift of the Spirit, we can find the self-control to go where we should instead of where we were headed. It's like taking my dog for a walk and telling him to "leave it" when he really, really wants to roll in deer excrement. If I didn't direct his senses away from nature's temptation, his desires would get the best of him, he would taint himself and come home needing to be purified before he could romp through the house again. We have to train ourselves to ask God to help us "leave it" before the brain lets the soul give into desires that have us rolling in habits that taint our relationships at home. It is prudent to ask God to purify us before we need purifying.

The only sex education I had from a religious standpoint was a cartoon filmstrip in fifth grade that had nothing to do with the holiness or emotion of it all. The mode of teaching used was more like the *Dragnet*[9] TV series in which police detective Sergeant Friday

---

9 Jack Webb, *Dragnet*, Television Series, Jack Webb (Los Angeles: MCA TV, 1951)

wanted as little drama as possible, asking his witnesses for just the bare facts of the matter. Since the fifth grade everything I'd been exposed to concerning sex came from the world with no mention of God. Being "of the world" when I got married, I had no concept of physical intimacy being defined as holy and sacred in God's eyes. Maturing spiritually brought me to want to understand His stance on sexual values and intimacy in comparison to those posed by pop culture. He already changed my heart in other areas of life with wonderful results. God tells us to "pray in all things." So I began. Paving the physical union with my loving husband with lots of prayer and God's grace allows me to receive my spouse in the holiness and love God intended. I thank Him for this gift of my husband.

For Christmas 2011, Husband surprised me by having our 1989 wedding video converted to DVD. During the holiday downtime, we sat together and watched our ceremony for the first time in a long time. It was with fresh ears and eyes that I watched and heard the words spoken at our Mass. It was celebrated for us, a new husband and a new wife taking vows within the Sacrament of Matrimony. I'm ashamed to admit that in 1989 that meant little to me. As I viewed the DVD, I was mesmerized by the prayers, the readings, and all the blessings called down upon us as we entered into our marriage covenant. I realized that all of those blessings "took" despite my ignorance of God's grace on our wedding day. I thank God that the eyes of faith opened my heart to gradually look for and accept each grace He bestowed upon this husband and this wife.

EYE-OPENER #2:   *God's law and civil law do not always mesh.*

Surprising as it is to some, God is pro-choice. Free choice, or free will, is another one of God's inventions:

It was He who created humankind in the beginning, and He left them in the power of their own free choice. If you choose, you can keep the commandments, and to act faithfully is a matter of your own choice. Before each person are life and death, and whichever one chooses will be given. He has not commanded anyone to be wicked, and he has not given anyone permission to sin. (SIRACH 15:14-15, 17, 20)

He created humans with the freedom to choose, and this liberty is protected by law in our country. We have this autonomy, but God expects us to make informed choices wisely and in prayer. As our children grow to make independent decisions, it is prudent that they have an understanding that, while the government protects one's right to choose, legal does not automatically equate to moral. God created us with a conscience to promote ethical decisions in the face of controversy. It is the duty of the decision maker to properly form that conscience by seeking knowledge surrounding an issue. We are constantly fed facts, figures, and opinions of the news affecting our town, city, state, country, and world. In the morning, we check the news headlines, hear radio reports while driving, and watch the 6:00 p.m. sound bites when we settle in for the evening. We are moved to pursue more details on current events that capture our interest or touch us personally. Similarly, we should take the time and effort to research the Church's verdict on modern morality topics because it is not often broadcast in our daily feedings.

The "everybody's doing it" mindset is not reserved for teenagers, but adults can take on this mentality as well. Many sincere people mistake preferences, conveniences, and peer approval for justification to dismiss some Church teachings as passé. When the choice is made to reject a teaching, the decision was very likely made without seeking the details behind WHY the Church stands by the decree. The common judgment that the Church is out of touch with today's people does not give weight to the Spirit-inspired longevity and wisdom of the Church's leadership, nor to the time and prayerful process involved before making a declaration, which draws its life from the teachings of Christ. My favorite version of the song, "The Music of the Night,"[10] from *Phantom of the Opera* includes two sentences describing the need to keep our eyes closed to avoid seeing the fullness of the truth; it makes life so much easier when we keep our eyes closed and remain in the dark. The words struck me as describing the indifferent rebellion with which many choose to forego Church pronouncements in certain areas. If we don't dig too far into the Truth, it becomes easier to make the Truth fit a preferred, whittled-down version of it, which better caters to our own desires.

In my pre-Christ life, I was one of those members who ignored much of what the Church declared. I am now a Christian sincerely wanting to live life as God would have me live it. In doing so, it has been my task to find out WHY the Church says WHAT it says about any debate. I trust in the Spirit-inspired wisdom the Church possesses, and I value the input from the Church's perspective to help me understand an issue from this angle.

Our maturing children lack exposure to God's side of the coin, which is centered on moral implications, regarding current affairs filling the airways and newspapers. Responsibility falls upon parents, in conjunction with guardians and religious educators, to provide this flip side. Alternately, dialogue takes place in public schools and among peers, usually providing only the secular version because, to be politically correct, it is highly recommended that God be mentioned only on private property. Young minds are similarly influenced by observing the popular, TV star, advertised point of view, which typically lacks influence from a Godly perspective. If a child

---

10 Andrew Lloyd Webber, "The Music of the Night" (Recorded by Michael Crawford, 1986) on the Premier Collection – Best of Andrew Lloyd Webber, Compact Disc (Polydor Ltd.: UK, 1988, The Really Useful Group PLC, 1988), for MCA Records

wants to "fit in," the trendy stance is easier to accept than question. A teen not having a strong relationship with God is often embarrassed to promote His view, and God is left out of conversation. Jesus would have had a quieter life had He left His Father off the agenda. Some loved Christ for the Truth, but others hated Him for it. He could have denied everything He stood for in order to save Himself and "fit in," but He spoke the Truth despite the consequences. He suffered for it. He died for it. I wonder how many today are strong enough to overcome mocking to defend God's side of Truth. How many are even aware of what He has to say? The sad part is that our young ones, along with many adults, don't realize they are ill informed when it comes to God's take on the morality of it all.

Some of the ongoing moral debates include:

1. **Embryonic stem cell research**

Those supporting embryonic stem cell research argue for the potential to regenerate diseased tissue in humans with the hope of future cures. This viewpoint shows much compassion for people suffering with debilitating diseases or injuries from accidents.

Those opposing embryonic stem cell research also possess compassion for those suffering with the burdens of disease and injury. However, this argument opposes the use of embryos, thereby also offering compassion to the unborn children of God whose lives are just as sacred as those seeking cures. Embryonic stem cell research is sustained by the abortion of unborn babies in order to obtain the stem cells. Those concerned for the lives of the unborn emphasize that medical science has made tremendous strides in stem cell treatment by successfully using umbilical cord and adult stem cells. The embryonic results have been flawed to date. There is no need to market aborted children when umbilical and adult stem cells are already capable of fulfilling the research needs of medical science.

2. **Abortion**

The moral debate over abortion is long-standing. When I was a twenty-something, uninformed Christian, the political phrase "pro-choice" became very popular. I did not know that pro-choice, as defined in the political arena, was a pretty way to say pro-abortion. Here and there, I would hear friends or acquaintances proclaiming to be pro-choice. It sounded fine to me. Everyone should be for choosing. I soaked in the merry slant of pro-choice like a sponge. I was so uninformed about either viewpoint of the abortion debate that when I became aware that pro-choice meant pro-abortion, there was no emotional impact. Due to this lack of knowledge, I had not formed a moral compass.

My interest in whether life began at conception peaked in the early nineties after viewing photos published in an old *LIFE* magazine I borrowed from Rebecca. She had a copy of a 1965 issue of the publication, which featured a piece entitled "The Drama of Life Before Birth."[11] The front cover and the article itself contain photos taken by Lennart Nilsson. Mr. Nilsson's photos were a milestone in giving the world a first glance at the developing human embryo from conception to birth. The vivid pictures struck me as I viewed the tiny embryo changing so dramatically on a very tight time line. The photo of the 18-week-old fetus sucking a thumb genuinely tugged at my heart strings. Recently, I re-read the article to see if any position had been voiced concerning pro-choice versus pro-life. Although the article did not mention any stance on abortion, it opened with a statement concurring that the birth of a human life takes place at the moment of fertilization. This public acknowledgment of a human life in the womb at the moment of conception might very well be edited out of the article if written in today's political climate.

---

11 Lennart Nilsson, "The Drama of Life Before Birth," *Life*, April 30, 1965

It was shortly after I began my Bible reading sessions at home that I came upon the following Scriptures referencing sacred life in the womb:

When Elizabeth heard Mary's greeting, the child leaped in her womb. And Elizabeth was filled with the Holy Spirit and exclaimed with a loud cry, "Blessed are you among women, and blessed is the fruit of your womb. And why has this happened to me, that the mother of my Lord comes to me? For as soon as I heard the sound of your greeting, the child in my womb leaped for joy." (LUKE 1:41-44)

For it was you who formed my inward parts; you knit me together in my mother's womb. (PSALM 139:13)

Before I formed you in the womb I knew you, and before you were born I consecrated you. (JEREMIAH 1:5)

There is so much to absorb from the Scripture in Luke describing Mary's visit with Elizabeth. Not only are words exchanged between these two pregnant women, but there is an exchange between the two unborn babies. Elizabeth is six months pregnant with John the Baptist. Jesus, who was just conceived prior to Mary's visit, is recognized by John from within Elizabeth's womb. Not only did the Holy Spirit grace the women, but it was by the Spirit that unborn John knew that his cousin, Jesus, in the womb next door was special. John leapt for joy. A tiny, six-month-old unborn baby jumping for joy within his mother's womb! Woman today, allowing a baby to live for six months within the womb, feel that same leap for joy. (Ok, sometimes it seems like a kick in the pants.) At any rate — that unborn baby is alive and leaping. Christ is the perfect example. Mary, John the Baptist, and Elizabeth knew that the child Mary was carrying was the Lord. Unborn Jesus already had the Savior knit into Him. He was already who He was supposed to be from within Mary's womb. Likewise, Elizabeth and her husband, Zechariah, knew that the baby Elizabeth was carrying was a prophet. It is the same with each of us. God knits within us the person we are to become from the moment of conception, and we begin the development process within the womb. After birth, the abilities He bore into us are, ideally, groomed and brought to full light. Unlike Jesus and John, we sometimes let the world get in the way of filling the shoes God cobbled uniquely for each individual.

I had a conversation once with a young-adult cashier ringing up my sale in a health food store. Somehow we got on the subject of abortion. I voiced my pro-life opinion and she informed me she was pro-abortion. This young woman went on to tell me how a fetus is not viable life because it could not live on its own. My calm reply was that if you left any baby, born or unborn, no matter what age, on its own to fend, the baby would die. As a matter of fact, if I locked her in a room somewhere and cut off her food supply, she would not be viable either. I left the store praying she would someday consider that a tiny human begins being at conception.

3. Divorce

There is definitely a wide gap between civil law and God's law when it comes to divorce. The Scripture verse that sums up the difference between the two views on divorce is found in the Gospel of Matthew. Jesus teaches much about both marriage and divorce within the verses below:

> *Some Pharisees came to him, and to test Him they asked, "Is it lawful for a man to divorce his wife for any cause?" He answered, "Have you not read that the one who made them at the beginning 'made them male and female', and said, 'For this reason a man shall leave his father and mother and*

be joined to his wife, and the two shall become one flesh? So they are no longer two, but one flesh. Therefore what God has joined together, let no one separate. They said to him, "Why then did Moses command us to give a certificate of dismissal and to divorce her?" He said to them, "It was because you were so hard-hearted that Moses allowed you to divorce your wives, but from the beginning it was not so. And I say to you, whoever divorces his wife, except for unchastity, and marries another, commits adultery." (MATTHEW 19:3-9)

Marriage is a vocation blessed by God. It is His design that this holy bond between a couple result in pure love and commitment founded on a loving bond with God. As it was in Moses' day and is now, unfortunately, many marriages do not live up to this ideal for one reason or another. Moses allowed divorce because of the stubbornness of his people. God, in contrast, intended that no man pull apart what He joined together. These opposing positions on breaking the marriage vow remain in our culture. It also remains that God puts up with our being "hard-hearted" in many matters of the human way. As shown throughout history, He recognizes that stubbornness leads us to play by our own rules, but He continues to love us unconditionally. He will forever pour out His grace upon us, working to draw us to the wisdom of His ways verses doing things our own way.

Divorce in our modern world is such a routine and acceptable custom of society that most people don't believe there is anything to debate. Popular opinion aside, there is disparity between our divorce court system and God's system when it comes to pulling asunder. Divorce is a man-made decree — Moses' law — that legally breaks the marriage contract. God's law does not offer such a decree.

Divorce is a sad social reality, and the Catholic Church comprehends the pain of those involved in civil divorce. The Church recognizes that when couples decide to separate, many seek divorce as a necessity to sever the legalities intertwined with the cultural responsibilities taken on with marriage. For examples: tax filings, credit ratings, future debts, health insurance, and a legal divorce is required to obtain a license to remarry. The Church offers counseling to its members suffering the consequences of divorce to assist in the emotional and spiritual healing process. By Divine decree, the Church cannot, however, recognize divorce as dissolving a marriage vow taken before God. Despite the unpopularity of the Church's policies regarding divorce and remarriage, it continues to uphold Christ's confirmation that divorce does not leave one free to remarry.

It would have been much easier to skip the issue of divorce because most non-Catholic, Christian denominations choose to follow Moses' law by allowing divorced couples to remarry within their church. This is quite contrary to how the Catholic Church proceeds with those wishing to remarry if either or both individuals have been divorced. There are divorced Catholics who leave the Church specifically because She will not remarry them prior to approval granted through the long, thorough investigation of annulment proceedings. When granting annulments, the Church does not claim power to dissolve a marriage joined by God. However, with wisdom and compassion drawn from the mercy of God, the Catholic Church has an annulment tribunal that hears the cases of Catholics whose marriages have failed. The process is meant to determine if the marriage vow that appeared valid at the time of the wedding, is found to have been flawed. The tribunal may determine that one or both of the parties did not freely enter into the marriage covenant the way God intended. An example would be a "shot gun" wedding where a pregnant teen marries out of fear or the parents pressured the couple to wed. Another example perhaps would be that one spouse revealed *after* vows were taken that he or she had no intention of having children. Not all cases submitted for an annulment are granted one. An annulment differs from a divorce in many ways, but I will not aim to explain the complexities of this decree. There is ample information available on the topic including in the Catechism and through the Vatican's website. This is an often misunderstood subject, and I encourage everyone with questions, concerns, or bitterness over the mysterious annulment process to research the issue from the horse's mouth – the Catholic Church.

My decision to include the topic of divorce was based on a recent conversation I had with a friend. That dialogue convinced me that there is still a great deal of confusion with respect to the Church's upholding of Christ's teachings regarding divorce. My friend, Dolores, is not Catholic. She was telling me about the wedding ceremony of her niece, which was a second marriage. Her niece is a former Catholic, divorced, and then remarried in her second husband's non-Catholic church. In Dolores interpretation, her niece joined her husband's denomination because she was "excommunicated" from the Catholic Church after getting divorced. In response to my friend, I informed her that her niece would not be excommunicated for being divorced. Divorced Catholics are able, and encouraged, to continue to fully participate in church life including the sacraments. It is when the divorced Catholic, still married in the eyes of God, remarries without an annulment decree that the person should not receive the sacrament of the Eucharist. This is the same requirement for anyone veering from any of God's laws in such a serious matter.

Every couple wanting to marry must obtain a marriage license from the state government. After being legally licensed, many Christian couples choose to have a church wedding. Unfortunately, some of those same couples seek a divorce in the future. Even though they took vows before the Lord, many do not think it necessary to face Him to break that same oath. Instead, they accept the power of the civil court to disavow promises made before God. Society, in general, ignores Christ's reminder that a marriage vow taken before His Father is a permanent bond. As a Catholic, I was married, with God as my witness, by a priestly representative of His Church. I would find it prudent to also go before Him through His representatives within the Church if ever finding myself in the turmoil of a legal separation. In my pre-Christ life, I would have been a person that skippcd past God straight to the civil court, but now I would take my pain and sorrow before Him in such a difficulty. Thankfully, it was my growth into an adult of God during my "formative years" of marriage that brought me to treasure the covenant with my husband and all that God intends within matrimony. Both the high divorce and high annulment rates speak to how broken our concept of entering into the marriage bond has become. Our God is all merciful, and I'm sure He pities our children caught up in a culture that has embedded divorce and remarriage as a standard procedure in the cycle of life.

Young adults would reap the benefits if steered toward inviting God back into the courtship and decision-making process that leads to a sacred marriage vow. If both partners would turn themselves over to Him and embrace the reality of God in the realities of marriage, abundant graces would assist the couple in learning and progressing together in unselfish love. In this surrender to Him, perhaps more and more troubled marriages would make it through the "worse." Praying hand in hand, God's grace has the power to transform marriage into the "better" to become what God intended – an unbreakable, true love for better or worse, through sickness and in health, to love and to cherish, and for richer or poorer, till death do us part.

No, unfortunately, God's law and civil law do not always mesh. This is precisely why adults have the responsibility to properly form their consciences concerning what God expects so they may nurture the young with information. We are failing our children when we forget or don't bother to teach all that was handed down by God. Parents are assigned by Him to share His Word, His Son, His love, and His ways with their children, His children. It's for the children's, the parents', the families', and the societies' health and well-being, not His.

GOD EXPECTS ME
TO PERSEVERE
IN PRAYER

First of all, then, I urge that supplications, prayers, intercessions, and thanksgivings be made for everyone. This is right and is acceptable in the sight of God our Savior, who desires everyone to be saved and to come to knowledge of the truth. (1 TIMOTHY 2:1, 3)

God expects us to offer prayers, petitions, and thanksgivings for everyone. As we are told in Timothy, by participating in prayer for ourselves and others, we assist God in His will that everyone may have eternal life. Since God encourages us to pray for everyone and it is pleasing to Him, we can expect and trust that when we place a petition before Him, He will answer those prayers. Using human terminology, He sometimes says "no," sometimes "yes," and sometimes He says "not yet, but keep praying." The hardest times are when it seems like he says nothing at all. With faith and perseverance we know He is listening and answering in His all-knowing, perfect-timing way, which is beyond our understanding.

Pope Benedict XVI gave a talk at a general audience in St. Peter's Square in Rome on May 25, 2011. He discussed the Scripture account where Jacob had a nightlong, physical, painful struggle with an unknown man (Genesis 32:22-32). After Jacob submitted to the stranger, the man blessed Him and left. Jacob came to realize he was struggling with God. The Pope compared Jacob's fight with God to our own struggles in prayer as we ask God for His blessings in life.

God knows our every need, worry, and desire, but He wants us to go to Him in perseverance in our battles. He knows best what we truly need even when we don't see it. Sometimes our wait for the blessing of an answer is long, but perhaps God is waiting for our complete surrender in the matter.

EYE-OPENER #1: *Praying is an ongoing act of love for the wellbeing of others.*

Erin bears witness to a "yes" that God gave to many years of praying for the spiritual welfare of our family. This sister's prayers began long ago from a distance when she moved away from home to pursue life, liberty, and happiness. She grew to understand her faith from a much more personal, Spirit-driven force than any other family member had discovered thus far. All she could do from afar was pray that we would each embrace the personal side of the Father, Son, and Holy Spirit. With much prayer behind her, God eventually answered "yes" to Erin. Bit by bit, she watched as our eyes spiritually opened. After waiting patiently for years, she was quite grateful for the outcome. Erin says we all began "dropping like flies" once Hannah had her spiritual awakening and began spreading the news.

A fondness for the Divine Mercy chaplet led me to incorporate this prayer for the ongoing needs of family and friends. When I receive the Eucharist at Mass, I often place my loved ones before God in prayer. My way of asking Him to take care of "my people" is to close my eyes and envision the person I am praying for at the feet of Jesus upon the crucifix. As I say the chaplet, I ask God to allow Christ's rays of love and mercy to shower that person with grace in his or her needs and struggles. One by one, I present each to God in this manner. Usually, I picture each individual with a solemn, prayerful, or sometimes nonchalant stance, which seems to reflect their comfort level with being taken to the cross in prayer. Once when I placed my husband underneath the cross, my mind's eye saw him begin to mimic taking a shower underneath the rays of light beaming forth from Christ. He would lift one arm up as if he were scrubbing his armpit, and then switch to the other arm, and yes, he was joyfully singing in the shower. In the quiet of the church, I suppressed my laugh. This is the way God equipped my husband, with a humor that helps him get through any of the difficulties he may be facing.

As you know, one of my family's long-term prayer requests has been for the physical and spiritual wellbeing of my brother with bipolar disorder. Andy is a man whose faith never left him, but he left the faith. My guess is that he no longer feels worthy to put himself before God, and so he stays away. He also fears trusting that his faith is real and not a figment of his disorder's imagination. This worry developed after he once rediscovered his faith during a manic episode 30 years ago. His devotion during such an agitated state was exaggerated and not based on reality. Likewise, choices made within mania were not his own, but stemmed from the illness. He once walked into heavy traffic believing God wouldn't let anything happen to him. An extreme example of the loss of reality was the episode when he truly believed he was the Son of God.

Andy is a man of high intelligence with astute awareness, a deep thinker, and he has a good sense of humor. His God-given talents lay hidden under a shroud of godlessness for a long time. His experiences kept him from pursuing spiritual health while he embraced the destructive habits of drugs and alcohol. Finally after many long years of sadness and hope for a change in his lifestyle, transformation in my brother became detectable. As the prayers continue, the "not yet" mode seems to be turning the tide. Fifty plus years of a mother's prayers, joined with the prayers of siblings and countless others, are bearing fruit. In 2006, within the grip of a severe manic episode, Andy was able to kick his addictions. The miracle is that from the difficult state of mental illness, physical addictions were overcome.

The shroud has been removed and the real Andy is being unveiled. Through his own experience of living with mental illness, my brother developed true empathy for other people in the same boat. He is able to relate to them, offer encouragement, and lend an open ear. One recent winter, when wind chills pushed the temperatures below zero, he took in a homeless man to get him out of the cold. Andy understood the man through his own battle with mental illness, living on the edge, and through a fear of being rendered homeless himself.

Andy's concern for the underdog was again seen after he ascertained that a customer frequenting the store was unable to read. During a conversation, Andy nonchalantly offered to teach the man this skill. After the initial shock of someone seeing through his guise, the gentleman accepted the offer. The two began meeting about once a week to obtain their goal. Andy enjoyed the task very much and told me it lifted him up to be able to help this guy. I think he discovered a great secret of life. That is, when we reach out to others and genuinely give of ourselves, we are lifted up by the exchange. We are at our finest while serving others unselfishly because it enables us to go beyond our own cares and woes. The Creator designed all of us to live in this cycle of helping and depending on each other. It is in loving others that we best reflect the image of God.

Andy manages well with proper medications, which balance his brain chemistry so he can live and work without high anxiety as a constant companion. The prayers, however, will not stop and are now focused on his choosing to stay clean and respond to God. It's a daily choice.

EYE-OPENER #2: *Perseverance is necessary because God never promised life would be easy.*

In Scripture, Jesus tells about the widow who persevered in her request for justice from an unjust judge:

Then Jesus told them a parable about their need to pray always and not to lose heart. He said, "In a certain city there was a judge who neither feared God nor had respect for people. In that city there was a widow who kept coming to him and saying, 'Grant me justice against my opponent.' For a while he refused; but later he said to himself, "Though I have no fear of God and no respect for anyone, yet because this widow keeps bothering me, I will grant her justice, so that she may not wear me out by continually coming." And the Lord said, "Listen to what the unjust judge says. And will not God grant justice to his chosen ones who cry to him day and night?" (LUKE 18:1-7)

All of us go through difficulties and have needs that don't seem to go away even after persistent praying. Don't lose heart! God promised us a rose garden, but not until life ever-after. In the meantime, we have been given a garden like Gethsemane, a garden, at times, full of agony. Yet, it is also a place full of joy, serenity, beauty, love, laughter, and a taste of heaven.

It is imperative during hard times to pray with perseverance. We can be revitalized by observing Christ. He did not live an easy life. As a man, Jesus went through the same emotions, temptations, physical ups and downs, struggles, and joys that we go through, yet without giving into sin. He was born to the world a pauper instead of a king. As an adult, He lived life on the road, traveling to spread the Gospel. Everywhere He went He was controversial and not welcomed by all. Those who did accept Jesus sometimes overwhelmed Him with their need to get to Him. This lifestyle at times left Him exhausted and emotionally drained, and He went off somewhere to be alone and recoup. Then there was agony, beatings, mocking, crowning with thorns, and hanging on a cross. Through all of Christ's human drama, look at how He always turned to the Father with plenty of prayer. He lived showing us how to live. We must learn to imitate Christ by running to the Father for help in hardship and also in joyful thanksgiving. We can do it. The Bible tells us so.

The cry of Jesus from the cross, "My God, my God, why have you forsaken me?" (Matthew 27:46), leaves many sure that Jesus felt abandoned by His Father while He suffered. This never sounded quite right because I was taught that God would never abandon His people, and that through faith we know He is there even in the worst of times. Jesus understood that better than anyone. How could it be true that He despaired? I've since heard insight that Jesus' words did not indicate abandonment, but rather He was "singing" from the cross. He was quoting the first verse of Psalm 22 of the Old Testament, which is a hymn of hope. Psalm 22 is a plea for help to get through the suffering of life. It begins in anguish, but by the end of the psalm, God's mercy is apparent; it is acknowledged that He heard the cries and did not turn away. The promise of Christ as Savior is also depicted in the verses. It finishes by giving all glory and praise to the Lord. The Jewish witnesses hearing Christ's cry would have been very familiar with the passage He quoted. Jesus was consoling them from the cross to have hope in the peace and joy of God's promise of salvation. Persevere because it will all work out in the end.

My sister, Josie, is an example of a woman who has not had an easy life. No one would blame her if she felt abandoned by God more than once over the course of life, but she remains a person of faith. She perseveres. A praying woman, she appreciates the love shown as our family offers many prayers for the needs of her family. She is the first to admit that God always takes care of her through thick and thin. She sees it clearly.

Josie epitomizes Christ-like compassion. This was most evident in the line of work she chose as a nursing assistant for the elderly. Over several decades, she has served each and every fragile patient with the respect they deserve. She once told me that there is something about cleaning and caring for someone's wounds that keeps her in the field. Her specialty is people. They are drawn to her because she is genuinely a good listener. She possesses a special intuition and understanding of the hurts that others carry. Her gift of compassion is given freely; the resultant good fruit cultivated from the depths of difficulty.

After facing years of escalating problems relating to her husband's alcohol habits, my sister gathered her courage, along with her four teenagers, and left home. This time she couldn't go back. The five stayed in a motel for a few nights. At this point, she had not been employed outside the home for quite awhile. Without a source of income, the expense of even a cheap hotel could not go on. A woman acquaintance understood the needs of Josie's family because she fled from a similar domestic situation. She owned an abandoned house in a bad neighborhood and offered it as refuge. Mother and children accepted the roof over their heads, huddled together, took strength from each other, and hoped for hope to arrive.

In an effort to provide a healthier environment for the desperate five, Rebecca and her husband, Joseph, invited the family to live with them and their three children. Joseph proudly announced he now had seven children. Not that this joint venture was ideal. It was not. Anytime two families merge with entirely different habits and ideas of running a household, there are things to iron out. Somehow they made it work. It was a home full of faith, hope, and love. Faith prompted all into prayer for guidance and endurance. Hearts were laid on the table with trust that God has control, now and into the future. Love flowed from Rebecca and Joe as they provided a home and served as a loving, caring example of what marriage can be between husband and wife. This brings us to hope. Hope that both sets of parents and children would accept God's graces enabling them to squeeze the good out of all that seemed so wrong. Hope that the children's estranged father would seek help to battle his addictions. The mantra is prayer and perseverance.

During the thick of it, Josie could not utter a single prayer from her lips or her mind. God took the words from her aching soul and heard every syllable. Life has been more than rough, yet she does not curse God. She has grown closer to Him as she looks back and marvels at the way He carried her through the muck. After being hired at a nursing home close to where she was living with Rebecca and Joe, she told me about an experience she had at work. The atmosphere at the institution was continually stressful due to a shortage of workers and the lacking ethics of some employees regarding human dignity. On a day when Josie was just about to lose it, she was given a burst of spiritual energy. The day started out bad and she was having trouble holding back tears. She had not broken down to cry, but it was still early in the shift. Her next task was to take an elderly woman to the chapel for reflection. Inside the chapel, she stood behind the resident's wheelchair and waited as her patient silently prayed. Josie took in the quiet of the chapel with a deep breath. Looking up at the cross, she confided in Jesus that she desperately needed a hug. Immediately she received an all-over "pins and needles" feeling. He squeezed her tightly. There was no need to cry. It was a good day.

Transformation has taken place over the period of post-traumatic stress that accompanies family upheaval. This mother of four now has a true calm about her. The peace comes from her firm belief that God has been guiding and providing as he promises. After two years of sharing another family's house, Josie was grounded enough to move into a rental house where she could raise her fledglings and begin another stage in life. As the next few years passed, Josie made great strides in picking up the reigns of responsibility that come with making a living, paying the bills, keeping a car running, and parenting from all angles. As her children have all left the nest, in early 2015, Josie kept a longtime promise to herself. She finished the proper schooling and passed the state tests to become a Certified Nursing Assistant. Diligence in prayer will continue for Josie and her family. After all the disorder and stress, we don't know what's stuck inside the heads and hearts of her young-adult children that has not been dealt with yet. That's the hardest part to help. Perseverance is necessary. We all continue to pray.

This same resolve in faith and prayer is evident in my sister Emily, her husband, and their three offspring who agree that life can be wearisome. They battled financial difficulties, job insecurities, foreclosure, and plans that go awry by packing their belongings, leaving unnecessary luxuries behind and moving in with Hannah. Their faith did not decrease through the storms, but had them seeking higher ground through the Lord to avoid drowning. As their situation forced them to simplify, they were challenged to put a plan in place to remove some debt and expenses. In the meantime, God's graces were apparent through Hannah who opened her home to them. As was the case when Josie moved in with Rebecca and Joe, it wasn't easy. Thankfully, Hannah and her temporary borders joined voices in prayer rather than donning boxing gloves. As finances permitted, after a couple years, Emily's family was able to take leave of "The House of Hannah", and they moved into a cozy rental house. It is most apparent that prayers were answered because everyone is still speaking to one another!

EYE-OPENER #3:   *The answer to prayer may await a response to God's voice by the person being lifted up in prayer.*

We all pray for people we know who don't share the same faith-filled enthusiasm as the one doing the praying. Praying for the needs of others includes asking that they open themselves up enough to become aware of God's grace.

I pray for my friend, Terri. Every once in a while we call each other to catch up. When my Dad's cancer was diagnosed, I called Terri to talk. She listened. My friend cried as I cried. She has a compassionate heart with a sincere empathy toward others. Terri has never had much of a relationship with God; she simply says she isn't very religious. What I see in her is a person who reflects His image when it comes to loving thy neighbor, but she has not yet pursued the "love God above all else" element that goes hand in hand. A few years ago, she called to tell me she was volunteering at a local hospital as a "rehabilitation escort." Her duties were to transport patients via wheelchair to a therapy session and later return them to their room. During the few moments the ride takes, she talks to the patients, and she listens. Terri thrived in this volunteer atmosphere and found joy in serving her charges. She told me she didn't know what came over her. All of a sudden she couldn't help herself — she had to be a volunteer at the hospital. She laughed that if someone would have previously suggested that she try volunteer work, she would have told them (in overly strong language) that they were crazy. When Terri finished explaining, I shared my speculation. It was God. He was guiding her to put her gifts of gentle kindness and compassion to good use. If we can't figure out what He's telling us, He lets it bubble up inside until we can't help but act. Terri replied that maybe I was right. She may not realize it, but her heart opened to the pull of His grace. She responded to what God had written on her heart. My prayers for my friend include a request that she asks Him to help her get to know Him better. When she does, He will take her hand and lead her to see Him more clearly.

Of course, my mom is an example of a person who perseveres in trust that God hears our prayers. She has always fervently prayed for her children to stay close to our Maker. Eight out of ten have either matured in a faith they never deserted or have fervently returned. Andy and Jean are the two remaining estranged from church-going.

Like many, Jean's relationship with God never developed in a personal sense as she grew into adulthood. Maybe her faith remained stagnant because she had a rough childhood, and it didn't feel like He was standing beside her. Going through school in the sixties and seventies with learning disabilities and a stutter were big hurdles. In addition, there was the fact that some are cruel to those who appear different, and Jean was not exempt from this rule.

Despite her challenges, Jean had a heart full of love, which she shared generously when given the opportunity. Her gift has always been of a nurturing nature. In her teens she was in demand as a babysitter in the neighborhood. In high school, she enrolled in a child development class in which she interacted well with the preschool participants. In particular, this sister thrived around babies and had a natural disposition for giving tender loving care. I recently ran into the woman who taught that child development course. We hugged a warm hello and reminisced as she told me of the amazing change in my sister when she worked with the preschoolers. During classes, Jean was so steeped in giving full attention to the children that her stutter disappeared. The description that comes to mind is that of the transfigured Jesus as His glory shone before three of His disciples on the mountain.

Six days later, Jesus took with him Peter and James and his brother John and led them up a high mountain, by themselves. And he was transfigured before them, and his face shone like the sun, and his clothes became dazzling white. (MATTHEW 17:1-2)

In the midst of children, Jean was on top of the mountain and transfigured into a teen with confidence and joy. She glowed with His glory and love every time she cared for youngsters. Forty years later, she continues to use her nurturing personality at a day care center where she is employed. The shining joy she finds caring for these little ones is a gift from God, which she gives back as a gift to the children.

Jean's faith flickers within her. My prayers include that she will be moved to give God permission to stir the embers with His grace, sparking her to embrace Him fully once again.

My brother, Will, waited until the ripe old age of 50 to respond to God's call; the phone must have been ringing off the hook for years as the family sent gazillions of prayers up to heaven for Will's spiritual and physical health. Except for the occasional wedding, he had not attended Mass for going on 30 years. A believer in the childhood teachings about God, he is another one who didn't actively seek Him from an adult perspective.

As a teenager, Will started in the restaurant business by washing dishes and worked his way up to become a chef, a trade in which he thrives. For many years he lived and worked in California. By state law, leftover food could not be given to the local food bank or shelters. The health board was concerned about food poisoning occurring from leftovers. Despite the mandate that leftovers be thrown away for safety's sake, Will found a way to feed the homeless wandering near the restaurant. He obeyed the law and threw away food at the end of each day. However, he would first wrap the leftovers before gently laying them on the top corner of the dumpster. Like clockwork, the hungry homeless would find these gifts and remove them before Will arrived the next morning. The evening meal came to be expected.

On the surface, Will did not have an awareness of a personal relationship with his Creator. Even so, his caring nature flowed out of him to reveal God nestled inside his heart. I remember telling Will that he's further into his relationship with God than he thinks. He's a perfect indication that when love and compassion are sincere, they take the form of service to others. Will already had the "love thy neighbor" part of the commandment in motion. That was automatic for him, but like me, for a long time he forgot about "love God above all else." I suggested it was time for him to start talking to the Lord again.

Will relocated to Florida about eight years ago to accept an offer of employment in a different restaurant. At the time, I would describe his relationship with our Lord as lukewarm. Things have changed. Gone are the days when Mom would ask him, "Are you going to Mass?" every time he phoned. Her son's heart was opened to seek God again. He began by asking faith-related questions of those of us back home. Then he started attending Sunday Mass and looking for answers in books. The mustard seed of faith in Will's soul was sprouting and taking up root in fertile ground.

When my Dad was diagnosed with cancer in 2007, Will flew home to be with our family. During his stay, I had the opportunity to talk to him about our beliefs. We talked about the Holy Spirit. We talked about the history of the Eucharist. We talked some more. Afterwards, he commented, "Why didn't anyone ever tell me this before?" The answer to that is complex. Partly, I think, it is because we are taught in grade school and high school religious classes with age-appropriate material. We cannot possibly receive all there is to know about God, and comprehend it, in 12 years or less of childhood schooling. Then we drop out and stop learning. There comes a time when we must grow up and seek for ourselves.

Will began talking to a local parish priest about returning full-fledged to his faith. His formed conscience would not let him receive the Eucharist until he first received the sacrament of Reconciliation. He was a bit intimidated about the confession part due to 30-plus years with some questionable behavior in it. I assured Will that the priest would help him through it. If we are willing to take the plunge to run back to our Father, we will find that He welcomes us with His arms open wide.

The year 2010 brought more evidence of prayers resulting in transformation. Will took the plunge. He attended a reconciliation service during the Advent season and made his confession. The very next day he attended Mass and was able to receive his "first" Communion as an adult.

EYE-OPENER #4: *At times, we must get out of the way to let God's grace be seen by others.*

My brother, John, was a lukewarm Catholic when he married Brianna. She was born of a non-practicing, Catholic father and a Mormon, strongly anti-Catholic mother. Being raised in the midst of this background, Brianna was not Catholic and had no desire to be one. In the meantime, John's faith strengthened as he matured and became the father of three daughters. He tried to share his growing spirituality with his loving wife. She countered and questioned everything, and she did so in an irritated state. Thus began a story of perseverance in prayer and waiting by John that his wife would someday understand, and possibly share, his strong beliefs. Many times I'm sure he felt like the answer God was giving was "no" because of my sister-in-law's stubborn opposition to all he believed. It is difficult to wait so long and hold onto hope, but each day should be seen as part of God's unfolding, ultimate plan. Hints of transformation sometimes edge up to the surface, but may go unseen by the human eye. In Brianna's case, the "hint" was a one day, all of a sudden, lightning bolt type event. It did not go unnoticed.

At the request of his parish priest, John put the story of Brianna's conversion into written words. The following is his article, which appeared in the parish's church bulletin:

After too many years of demonstrating to my wife how a wishy-washy, uncommitted, cradle-Catholic behaves; I finally began to take seriously the faith that I had taken so lightly for so long. As I slowly progressed in my practice and appreciation of the great Catholic traditions and doctrines, I naturally wanted to share them with my wife. That's when things got complicated. I knew that I could not push my faith on her, but I was often impatient in understanding why she could not see the benefits that I was rediscovering. As a non-practicing, baptized Mormon who had more questions than answers, she agreed to raise our children as Catholics when we were married, and she dutifully kept her promise. She even went a step further by home-schooling them with a Catholic curriculum. All the while she attended Mass with us while yawning her way through. Try as I might, through prayer and persuasion, I could not bring her to embrace religion as any more than a nice practice to be relegated to Sundays and the occasional holiday. Her lack of faith and general understanding of the concept of "God" was a continuous source of frustration for me and a regular topic of discussion between us. Often the discussions became heated and did less to advance her understanding than to create a bigger divide between us. I remember clearly, after one such discussion, throwing my arms in the air as she left the room and acknowledging to God that I guessed we would never have the Catholic family that I had been hoping for.

In steps the Holy Spirit. Even as I despaired and washed my hands of it; we continued our practice of attending weekly

Mass and schooling the children as a semi-Catholic family. One of these, otherwise ordinary, Sundays, my wife had an encounter with the Holy Spirit that changed her life, and our family's, forever. As we entered the Church, she was stopped, barely inside; she recalls her breath being taken away. She remembers an overwhelming warm, calming sensation entering at her heart and flowing to her head, toes, and fingers and beyond. She describes it as a washing. All of her anxieties, fears, and doubts were removed, and she was overcome with peaceful warmth. I, as usual, was oblivious and had continued on (right church; wrong pew). I had to return to get her as I realized she was not following us. She tried to tell me what she was experiencing, but I was too concerned with getting to our seats. Only later was she able to get me to hear what she had experienced, and I still did not comprehend the magnitude of her experience. From that day on, she was definitely changed or maybe transformed. As I learned that my best role may be to get out of the way, she was off and running; propelled by the Holy Spirit. She began to devour any Catholic literature she could find and was soon able to explain to her family, friends, and to me, many precepts of our faith. Despite resistance by her family, disruptions in our daily routines, and two occasions where the RCIA program she was attending was unexpectedly canceled, she continued her pursuit of the Truth. After a couple of years, and finding a home at St. Thomas More, she was finally baptized into the faith, confirmed, and received the Eucharist for the first time at the Easter Vigil in 2005. I thank God for his persistence, "the Hound of Heaven," and for demonstrating to me what can be accomplished when I put my trust in Him or, at least, get out of the way.

Since Brianna's baptism in 2005, she has eagerly shared her discoveries with John, their daughters, and her parents. Her father absorbed the information and returned to the Catholic faith, but the rift between her mother, Rose, and her Church continued to be a source of conflict. As John had prayed many a prayer for his wife's conversion, Brianna in turn did the same for her mom. Rose's health deteriorated over these years, but she never budged on her arguments against Catholicism. Then, out of the blue, in the spring of 2011, she approached Brianna with a startling request for help to convert to Catholicism. Rose had a very vivid dream that was different than a typical night's dream. She explained to her daughter that Jesus came to her with His arms open wide. She accepted His invitation. At first Brianna and John believed it was ill health playing on Rose's mind, but after much conversation, they saw that her demeanor and heart had sincerely changed. Brianna and John took Rose to their parish priest to discuss this drastic about-face. After talking, the priest approved her wish to convert. Rose was received into the Church in June of 2011. She died the morning of July 6, 2011.

My own experience of stepping aside came early in my spiritual metamorphosis. It didn't take long for me to realize that gushing about discoveries got in the way while trying to share them with my spouse. My gusto did not motivate him into discussion since he considered religion a personal matter. So, I quit gushing. Instead, I turned to praying for the two of us to grow closer in our common faith. So close that someday we will clunk heads as we meet in the middle. I pray that we live out the rest of our marriage with Christ as the center of our household, not only in church or on Sundays, but every day. Not individually, but together.

It's been several years since my spouse shocked me while out on one of our Friday evening dates. Dinner arrived at our table, and Husband simply asked me to say grace with him before we ate. I wasn't ready for that kind of spiritual growth. The kind that is harder than displaying your faith at church where everybody is in sync. The kind that makes me squirm a little because most people don't say grace in restaurants. This from my guy who used to tell me he doesn't need to talk about it. Following my husband's lead, we adopted the habit of saying grace before each meal even when out in public.

Husband and I now meet in the middle more often than not as we continually grow in faith, hope, and love. One thing is for sure, none of us are ever meant to stop growing. It is a blessing to understand that God will always find ways for us to grow stronger, through Him, in our partnership of holy matrimony. I'm happy to step aside and allow God to lead our way.

EYE-OPENER #5:   *God often answers prayer through others — the "communion of saints."*

Several days before Dad died, I whispered my request that he somehow let us know if Jesus kept his promise. That same request was repeated by my niece Lainey in a Father's Day card she bought to give her grandfather, but he died the day before the holiday. She wrote him a message anyway believing that he could read it from everlasting life. The following was written in her note:

> *"Happy Father's Day, Papa! You got an amazing gift today; you got to meet God and Jesus. We miss you so much. I'm sorry this card was too late, but I wanted to tell you that I greatly admire you for your faith and your passion for your family. I know I want a marriage like yours and Grandma's: based on God. You were an amazing person and a loving grandfather. I may only have three living grandparents now, but I will always have 4 in my heart. I was fortunate enough to have*

you in my life for 18 years, and I thank God for it. I learned to play poker from the best, even though I know you <u>let</u> us win (and we only played with pennies). It will be hard, especially this Christmas, because I won't see you at the poker table as I turn the corner at Aunt Mary's and you won't be constantly asking me "Where are my cookies?" But we all know you'll be there with us just not in body. I made cookies for you, Papa. Maybe now you can taste them. I have so much more to say, but I am out of room. So I'll end it with this: Happy Father's Day, Papa. I love you, and I will miss you so much! And <u>please</u> let us know if Jesus kept his promise."

Love, Lainey
XXXX OOOO

We are all connected to one another as God's family, via prayer and His grace, within the communion of saints. We probably all know someone who believes God provided a comforting sign that a deceased family member is in His hands. My dad belongs to this communion of saints. My family firmly believes God allowed my father to encourage us in our faith with signs that he has been fulfilled in the promises of God. Let me share the story with you:

As a young man, Dad was trained in the field of grooming dogs. He eventually used his skills to establish his own grooming business to provide for his growing family. When he began this venture, his business was unique because he made house calls and spruced up the canines in the comfort of their own homes. Down the road, Dad turned our garage into a grooming shop where customers would arrive by appointment. Familiar with the majority of dog breeds, my father was most enamored with the Sealyham Terrier. Our first pet Sealy was quite a good looking female, so Dad took to competing her in dog shows. Of course, we thought she should have won all the time, but sometimes she came in second or third. Honesty forces me to mention that, in most shows, there would only be two or three Sealyhams competing because the breed is little known in the United States. This breed originated in Wales, and today is found mainly in the United Kingdom and South Africa. To put the scarcity of the Sealy into perspective, according to the American Kennel Club's website,[12] in 2006 (the most up-to-date statistics prior to my father's death in 2007), the number of registered Sealyhams in the U.S. was only 68 compared to 123,760 Labrador Retrievers.

All of us siblings eagerly accompanied Dad on his grooming appointments at one time or another. Hannah developed the same love for the trade that our father had, and she took over the enterprise when he retired. She has since done him proud in carrying on the family business. Hannah closed her shop for a week after Dad died in order to be with the family and help tend to matters. Once back to work, she received a call from a young man who just purchased a Sealyham puppy from a breeder in New York. He called to see if Hannah knew how to prepare it for the show ring. As a matter of fact, she knew quite well. She learned from her father, an expert at the time consuming, painstaking technique of stripping the coat by hand, to ready a Sealyham for competition.

Another phone call came in. This time from a married couple who purchased a Sealyham from the same breeder. The pups were siblings, but the owners did not know each other. The breeder mentioned to the couple that he sold another pup to a man living in their area. They contacted the young man hoping he could recommend a groomer for their Sealy. He recommended Hannah. Mind you, it had been a good 25 to 30 years since any customer presented a Sealyham for grooming. My sister was thrilled. All of a sudden she had two Sealyhams to groom when at first there were none. By the abundant grace of God, Dad used his favorite breed, a rare breed, to reach out to us in a way that would be interpreted as his voice.

---

12 akc.org

Another joyful "sign" was when Emily received a call from Dad in a dream shortly after he passed away. The phone rang, and she answered. It was Dad. She couldn't see him, but it was definitely his voice. It was stronger and more upbeat than it had been in a long, long while. He told Emily he called to let everyone know that he's doing just fine. Everything is all right. He could only talk for a minute, and then he said he had to get back. It was a good dream.

About a week after Dad's funeral, I got back into my daily walking routine with Zeus. It was good therapy for me, and I took to silently talking to my father while hiking through the woods. One beautiful, sunny day after walking, I sat down on a rock beside our pond waiting for Zeus to finish his swim. As I sat, a crystal clear, head-shot hologram of my father hovering over the water appeared in my mind. He was laughing. This was such an awesome, unexpected visual because Dad had always been a subtle grinner and a smirker, not a laugher. It was rare to see him laugh such a hearty one as he did that day by the pond. With that image fresh in my mind, I knew he was happier now than ever. Jesus kept His promise.

GOD EXPECTS ME TO SEEK HIM

So I say to you, Ask, and it will be given you; search, and you will find; knock, and the door will be opened for you. For everyone who asks receives, and everyone who searches finds, and for everyone who knocks, the door will be opened. (LUKE 11:9-10)

When you search for me, you will find me; if you seek me with all your heart, I will let you find me, says the Lord. (JEREMIAH 29:13-14)

God expects us to seek Him. Not just once, but every day. As we seek His presence in all we do, and find Him as promised, our earthly needs will not be a cause for such worry. He will see to our best interests. Unfortunately, while in the throes of the hustle and bustle of life, we tend to forget that He should be the most important, central part of existence. He is the air we breathe.

It has taken me a decade to put this book to bed and allow it to find its way into your hands. I thought back about the roller coaster ride I've had with my confidence levels over these years of writing. Some days I positively knew that finishing this manuscript was exactly what I should be working toward. Yet, I had a record of scolding myself for thinking God would have taken me seriously that day, so long ago, when I told Him I wanted to inspire others to seek Him by writing about His presence in my life. On and off, I convinced myself that ordinary people like me don't go around writing books. Even so, I never quit writing. I continued to pray hard for God to help me do what it was that He wanted done.

Through the doubts and ups and downs, I became aware that I was questioning God's one-on-one relationship with me in this particular matter. Many times, I prayerfully apologized to Him. After incidents of doubt, I would tell Him that it wasn't that I didn't trust Him. Rather, I didn't trust myself enough to know if He was truly leading me forward or if it was imagination. I told Him it wasn't Him; it was me. (Wow, that sounds like I was breaking up with God and trying to let Him down easy.)

Through the gift of self-awareness, I came to admit that my difficulty with unbelief was, indeed, because I did not trust *Him* fully. Had I done so, doubts would not have troubled me so often, and the days of angst would have been minimized. I had to give up my worry that even though I put myself in His arms, He may need to drop me for something more important. I knew that as His daughter, He personally looks after me in all my needs. My heart, however, did not always trust this personal touch, especially for something I thought of as being out of my realm. This awareness moved me to begin praying for the ability to trust fully that I am held tightly in His arms just for the asking.

In early March of 2015, Zeus and I took another long walk with God. I prayed and pondered. During that walk, it hit me that my prayers were being answered. I had progressed with those trust issues within the last year and even more so in the last few months. It is my belief that if God expects me to have full trust in Him, He will grant the grace I seek to do it. (Realistically, I may need to seek His help more than once because of human weakness, but at least I should recognize the need a little sooner.) After the fact, I clearly see His footsteps alongside mine providing everything I needed to get me to this point. He provided the gifts of people in my path who helped in various ways, grace to strengthen my faith, grace to persevere despite my doubts, and the peaceful and Spirit-filled walks with Him that took me to the mountain top in thought.

The realization came that all of these gifts were present, but my lack of trust didn't always allow me to fully accept them as progression. I have since become better at taking each day as a piece of His plan. Over the last several months, while working toward a publication deadline, I have been unusually calm rather than getting overly anxious about the long to-do list. One way or another, a new day would lead me closer to what God has in mind. Life plays out a day at a time for all of us. In a prayerful mode, it is my responsibility to do what is humanly possible with what life presents each day, and then I must let go of it. In the meantime, after letting go, I let God deliver the next day to me, and then I use my human element again to the best of my ability.

On a daily basis, I give the gift of myself to God, and I ask that He use me as an instrument in what it is He wants done. In trust, I believe He considers this a personal, precious offering. Even though some days my gift to Him is broken, or it looks like a child's portrait with colors outside the lines, I trust He will cherish and take care of the gift of me forever. He will put it to good use because it's a gift from His daughter, and it was given with the sincerity of love.

Before the walk was over that day, my thoughts were moved to pray part of Mary's Song, the "Magnificat," from Scripture in which Mary praises God:

> *My soul magnifies the Lord, and my spirit rejoices in God my Savior, for he has looked with favor on the lowliness of his servant. ... for the Mighty One has done great things for me, and holy is his name. (LUKE 1:46-49)*

The words did not come out exactly right, but for the first time in my life, I prayed Mary's Song from my heart. The significance of this for me is tremendous. Although I was very familiar with the

Magnificat, I always associated it as a prayer for Mary alone. It never crossed my mind to apply it to myself because it seemed arrogant to consider that God would do great things for me and look with such favor upon me. This day, the Blessed Mother's prayer had new meaning to me. I understood I was joyfully praising God for all the great things He has done for me over these years of seeking, finding, and growing up. He has looked with favor on me and has moved me to use my gifts and talents to share Him with others. This is what He wants to do with each of us.

In the womb, God knits into us gifts and talents telling of the person God created us to become. He expects us to grow up enough to share them with others in love and gratitude. It is not arrogant to admit to our strengths, but necessary so that we may go out and use them joyfully, and praise our Lord for the great things He will have us do in His name. Some of us will grow to share our talents with multitudes. Others will do so with one neighbor at a time. Either way, we have participated in our Lord's mission for the building up of the whole – the Body of Christ.

The more we seek about God, the more we come to understand that all He expects of us will not play out in the exact same way for you or me or someone else. Each individual is different and unique with their own capabilities and limitations. One thing God does not desire for any of us is to go it alone. He does desire that we love Him from the depths of our hearts. So much so, that love will move us to offer our gifts and talents for the sake of others.

Everything God expects is obtainable through Him. While seeking, count on Him and the gifts He provides: His Spirit, His Mother, His Church, and His people — the communion of saints — to draw forth the best of everything He put within you. Then as that long-lived quip goes, "There, but for the grace of God, go I."

I'm going out to walk now. God expects me.

ABOUT THE AUTHOR

The author's mother has been calling her by the nickname "Mayme" since she was a child. Mary Bulger presents this sentimental tag in her first book, *God Expects Me,* to honor her mother and family heritage. She delights in time shared with family and friends, dabbles in painting, has a passion for cooking up recipes geared toward healthy eating habits, and is active in the Catholic parish where she is a member. She currently enjoys a part-time position at a neighboring parish as the rectory cook. Mayme lives in Pittsburgh, Pennsylvania, where she always looks forward to a morning cup of coffee with her loving husband, Mark.*

www.gembymayme.com
gembymayme@gmail.com

---

* Official name of Husband; used by permission.

33136694R00153

Made in the USA
San Bernardino, CA
25 April 2016